Praise for Conversion

For further information contact AudioInk Publishing
+14255266480 or email support@AudioInk.com

Library of Congress Cataloging-in-Publication

Heathman, Bryan
Conversion Marketing: Converting Website Visitors into Buyers
p.cm.
ISBN: 978-1-61339-256-0
LCCN: 2012937639
1. Business & Economics/Marketing/General
2. Business & Economics/Economics/General
3. Business & Economics/Sales & Selling

Distributed by AudioInk Publishing
Cover Design by DeeDee Heathman
Interior Design by DeeDee Heathman

Printed in the United States of America

For volume discounts, contact AudioInk Publishing 1-425-526-6480

CONVERSION
MARKETING

Convert Website Visitors to Buyers

Bryan Heathman

AUDIO Ink
PUBLISHING

Dedicated to the top 3% of marketers on the planet....

Welcome to the club.

Table of Contents

Foreword to this Marketing Classic

When I started my work as an author and motivational speaker, I had a philosophy of helping people help themselves to achieve their dreams. Through this mindset, I have had the privilege of working with leading professional speakers and sharing the stage with US Presidents, professional athletes, famous CEOs and fighter pilots.

Through these life experiences, I have come to realize that life is less about what you accomplish, but it is more about who you help along the way.

Over the years, I have seen marketing tools come and go. Smartphones and social media have changed the landscape of marketing and the next disruption is right around the corner for marketers. What I enjoy about the philosophy of *Conversion Marketing* is that the principles hold true for decades, regardless of the latest marketing technologies.

Research reveals that consumers differ greatly in their needs and desires. Therefore, consumers must be classified into segments to properly market. In my social media endeavors, I have created distinct segments with my fans whether they are fans of my work in politics, inspiration or leadership.

A conversion strategy is a fundamental aspect to each of these segments. My thinking around what makes consumers buy has been shaped by Dan Ariely's book Predictable Irrational. *Conversion Marketing* takes these principles further by practically applying them to website marketing and delving into the psychological buying triggers that influence online purchase behavior.

Marketing is not a static endeavor. Marketing is constantly adapting to consumer buying patterns and *Conversion Marketing* is one of the revolutionary changes that keeps the marketing field alive and vibrant.

As you read this work on the subject of conversion, I think you will find that *Conversion Marketing* is a powerful tool for impacting the bottom line in many types of marketing endeavors, from start-ups to Fortune 500 companies.

Chris *Widener*
Author & Professional Speaker
Author of New York Times best seller *The Angel Inside*

THE ONLINE MARKETING ECONOMY

Have you ever heard the phrase, "What's old is new again?" No truer words were ever spoken when it relates to building a high-performance website to convert visitors into buyers. Whether you are talking about the hottest new style in designer jeans, auto body styles or handbags, styles come and go in predictable cycles. Much like the latest fashions, what is working on the Internet such as viral marketing, social media, sweepstakes, coupons, mail-in rebates and free shipping, has been working in the offline world for decades.

Before we get to work on your website conversion rates, let's start with a shocking-but-true history lesson.

Back in the 1995, when the hottest fashions were influenced by TV shows like *Friends*, the concept of eCommerce was brand new. Believe it or not, massive debate and speculation arose as to whether or not eCommerce would take hold. At this time, the multi-billion dollar eCommerce pioneer Amazon was a start-up with its employees working on doors that had been modified into desks. **Really!**

In 1996, I was sitting around a mahogany boardroom table with a group of razor-sharp marketers employed by small company owned by Bill Gates; a privately-held image licensing company called Corbis. We were having a heated debate as to whether or not to spend our resources building an eCommerce store. eCommerce was so new then, we actually decided AGAINST building an online store as the group didn't believe it was going to take-off. Really?

Being a Marketer when eCommerce was brand-new offers amazing perspective about how to structure websites for conversion given all the changing technologies used in online marketing. Currently, the leading eCommerce companies, such as Amazon, eBay, Dell, Apple iTunes and Netflix are transacting hundreds of billions of dollars in eCommerce sales each year, which is a long cry from the days debating whether the business model of eCommerce would stick.

Today, eCommerce opportunities exist like never before and these opportunities keep expanding! Companies I work with are using eCommerce to supplement their income, make a great living, or become spectacularly wealthy leveraging the techniques in this book. It is universally understood that the Internet was, and still remains, one of the fastest-growing marketplaces ever experienced in the history of the world. It is now possible to run a highly successful business virtually anywhere in the world.

Each year, I spend a month in a tropical location on a working vacation while running a publishing business. Because of a well-crafted Conversion Marketing strategy, the business never misses a beat. I am able to get online and manage my business affairs from a tablet and a laptop, while sipping an icy refreshment by the pool.

You too can pick and choose when and where you work by creating your own Conversion strategy.

The principles contained in this book include highlights of successful real-life Conversion Marketing campaigns, designed to stimulate ideas for your business. The goal of Conversion Marketing is to equip you with formulas for achieving success in converting Vistors into Buyers.

The experiences shared in this book come from running hundreds of promotional campaigns for leading companies such as Proctor & Gamble, Nissan Motors, Travelocity, CVS Pharmacy and AT&T. Timeless online promotional-marketing expertise, combined with the unique psychology of online Conversion Marketing, can be applied to any marketing organization or product strategy.

As you absorb the ideas presented in this book, you will see how various companies, like well-respected luxury brands BMW, Prada, and Gucci have successfully harnessed the selling power of automated marketing technology to leverage the Internet for their incredible profits. Business-to-business marketers will benefit from the resources, techniques and principles of Conversion Marketing as well. Small businesses equally benefit from learning these tools of influence, as a Conversion Marketing strategy can be deployed with minimal marketing budgets. The psychology of buying goods and services can be applied to your website using these easy-to-follow principles of conversion.

So let's breakdown *Conversion Marketing* into the fundamental building blocks. The magic of being a successful Conversion Marketer boils down to your Conversion Rate – your ratio of Visitors to Buyers. Did you know that less than 2% of typical website visitors complete a transaction? Did you also know that millions of websites receives only ten visitors a day? When you do the math, this translates to six online transactions per month. This is hardly compelling and is precisely the purpose of this book; for businesses with hundreds of millions of visitors per month to the small just getting started.

The primary goals of the Conversion Marketer are:

1. Increase Traffic to your website

2. Increase your Rate of Conversion from Visitors to Buyers

With these two primary goals in mind, let's explore some simple math to better understand the process.

Do you have any idea what a Visitor is worth to your website? On average, it can cost anywhere from $.30 to $275.00 to attract a first time visitor to your website. Perhaps your cost per visitor is significantly more if you sell business jets or luxury vacation homes, but stick with this example for a moment. Let's assume a first time visitor costs $2.00 per visit. This number needs to factor-in your time, your promotional and advertising costs, design work and overhead. If you are doing a great job and getting a 2% conversion rate, then each new customer you acquire is costing $100.00 per transaction, even if this customer spends $29.97 per transaction. Here's what that looks like:

> **$2.00** Visitor x **100** visitors = **$200**
> **100** Visitors x **2%** = **2** conversions
> **$200/2** = **$100** Cost/Conversion

It does not take a mathematical wizard to understand that you must do one of 3 things to fully capitalize on this fast-growing marketplace: 1) lower your cost per visitor; 2) increase your conversion rate; or, 3) increase your average purchase dollar value. By understanding the principles in this book, you will fully understand how to accomplish these goals simultaneously, using automation, so that you too can profit from your ideas and enhance your career success.

Many Internet marketers have three common weaknesses when designing their marketing strategy for higher conversions. If you already have an eCommerce website, see if any of these vulnerabilities sound familiar.

Weakness #1 - Audience Targeting: You're attempting to sell goods to your entire audience of traffic, versus segmenting your website Visitors. With these Conversion Marketing ideas, you will learn how to cater your efforts just to the Buyers by clearly identifying what makes them tick.

Weakness #2 - Single Campaign Optimization: You're spending your time sequentially, one marketing campaign at a time, to sell a variety of goods and services. In today's climate, your website will need to cater to multiple audiences simultaneously, which may require launching multiple marketing campaigns with highly specific targeting.

Weakness #3 - Catch-All Philosophy: The Design of your website and promotional messaging are a catch-all for multiple audiences. Ultimately, using a catch-all philosophy only "catches" a few.

In exploring your Conversion Marketing strategy, we will discover how to profile your target audience and increase your conversion rates. The common pitfalls listed above can be remedied with a Conversion

Marketing strategy that identifies and caters to the needs of your target audience.

Before we go further, it is important to understand the fundamental building blocks of the Internet economy by understanding how money flows online.

The Flow of Money

Money is made on the Internet in 4 primary methods:

Method #1: Publishing

A fundamental building block of all commerce on the web is inherent in the Publishing business model. Publishing starts with the fundamentals which are essential for understanding how revenue is generated online. We can start with the most basic component of Publishing – traffic and attracting Visitors. There are distinctions to understand how a Publisher thinks about their audience. Here is a high level breakdown:

- ✓ **Visitors** – A total count of how many times your website was visited in a period of time.

- ✓ **Unique Visitors** – Unique Visitors is a culled-down Visitor number to help you understand how many distinct individuals are coming to your website. This number typically represents the core of a buying audience, as it reflects the all-important Repeat Visitor.

- ✓ **Page Views** – Online publishers like to create a user experience encouraging multiple page views per visit. When a Visitor starts to click through the pages on your website, each new click to a new page is called a Page View.

✓ **Ad Views** – Ultimately, online Publishing companies (MSNBC, MTV, NYTimes, CondeNet and Yahoo!) measure their success by how many ads they can display to each unique visitor. Back in 1995, the mantra for each Ad View was "nickel, nickel, nickel" as each ad displayed earned a nickel in revenue on average. The value of an Ad View is significantly lower today on average and is measured by a fast-evolving list of metrics that are explored in coming chapters.

✓ **Click-Throughs** – Each time a Visitor clicks on a link or display ad. The overall performance of a Publishing website, ad or email is measured by how many Visitors click on on the ad.

✓ **Average time spent on website** – Finally, online marketers like to measure how much time each Visitor spends on their websites in order to benchmark the level of engagement and/ or appeal of content.

Method #2: Advertising

As a Conversion Marketer, your essential job is to get your website noticed and products/services sold. This is true of whether you are working on a start-up company or for a mega-brand such as Google, Coca-Cola, Nike, Starbucks, Microsoft, Facebook or Estée Lauder. The primary methods which marketers use to get noticed can include advertising and promotion. Marketing is sometimes explained in terms of Above-The-Line advertising and Below-The-Line promotional tactics. Above-the-line marketing is defined as mainstream media advertising and is somewhat weighted to what marketers define as "Branding" activities. Below-the-line advertising is defined by activities such as promotional marketing or viral marketing (often called Word of Mouth advertising).

Above the Line Marketing

Marketers use many different types of advertising and marketing communications for Above-the-Line activities, which include running terrestrial advertisements on TV, radio, newsprint, magazines and outdoor advertising (billboards, stadium advertising or bus stops). Online advertising includes CPM (cost per thousand) banners sometimes called "display ads", video interstitials (online video commercials viewed as you click-through to desired content), sponsorship, pay-per-click (PPC) and paid placement.

Below the Line Marketing

Below-the-line marketing means affordable yet efficient "call-to-action" marketing, reaching various target groups with promotional methods measured by the cost per response. Marketers can leverage their online advertising performance using Word-of-Mouth tactics such as viral marketing (which we explore in Chapter 5) to increase the effectiveness of their campaigns.

Basically, an advertising budget will be divided up into "buckets" which target the four key areas of the purchase process listed here.

- ✓ **Awareness:** Generating product or brand awareness via advertising or a public relations push.

- ✓ **Consideration:** Increasing active product consideration by engaging your target audience with relevant messages related to your products/services.

- ✓ **Channel Marketing:** Sales channel coverage in retail stores, trade shows, managing distributor relationships or partners who represent your products in certain channels of distribution.

- ✓ **Call to Action:** Closing the sale by getting the benefits of the product to hit home with your consumers, or what is called "Call-to-Action" marketing. Often, Call to Action marketing is referred to as Promotional Marketing.

Method #3: Promotion

When you are planning your online Conversion Marketing strategy, the first exercise is to know your basic marketing parameters, or the Four

P's, in order to understand which tools to use to capture revenues most efficiently.

Parameter #1 – Product: First, knowing why people are buying your Product is essential. Create a clear description that communicates its benefits and features, leaving no room for misconception. Have a vision of your product's utility to your audience firmly in your mind.

Parameter #2 – Price: The second parameter is Price. Pricing is an essential part of your marketing strategy. Pricing can be difficult to determine if you are introducing a new product to the market. If you want to read more about understanding pricing models, one good resource is *The Irresistible Offer: How to Sell Your Product or Service in 3 Seconds or Less* by Mark Joyner. Another excellent resource with innovating thinking on pricing is a book called *Predictable Irrationality* by Dan Ariely. I keep this book next to my desk at all times.

Parameter #3 – Place: The third factor is Place. The physical place of your product can also be defined as your distribution channels. The placement of your online message to generate conversions will directly impact the speed of your results.

Parameter #4 – Promotion: The fourth parameter is Promotion. In today's eCommerce climate, below-the-line marketing is the clear forerunner when creating online Conversions. Tools which are successful online have been used offline for decades, including:

✓ Coupons, price discounts

✓ Sweepstakes and Instant Win Games

✓ Event marketing

✓ Lead generation, such as free white papers, free trial, case studies and industry research

✓ Premium items such as unique pens, coffee cups, beer mugs, calendars, mouse pads or magnetized shopping list tablets.

So, what will YOU promote? Will you use a 50-percent-off sale, coupon offers, two-for-one specials or a targeted-sweepstakes offer? How about a free-trial period? Is my offer compelling enough? The answers to these questions are fundamental to the Conversion Marketer's success.

An important note is that some Promotional tools are not right for every company. If you market luxury items or manage a premium brand, such as Waterford Crystal, Rolex, Armani, or Mercedes Benz, then some promotional tools are likely not useful to you. Why? When you sell a premium-branded item, you use the allure of the brand image to draw buyers to your company. Consider running branding campaigns, event sponsorships and paid celebrity endorsers, which are of high value to keep your brand image top-of-mind with your audiences.

If you manage consumable products such as bottled coffee drinks, digital cameras or dry cleaning services, then promotional tools are proven to generate cost-effective sales conversions. Products that are in highly competitive categories or are high-impulse items benefit greatly from the visibility that promotion creates. Business-to-business promotional offers are almost universally effective in generating qualified leads into your sales channel(s).

Method #4: Branding

New and established companies alike need to build the bond of TRUST when planning to convert website traffic into revenue. One study by the Harvard School of Business shows that a consumer needs three to seven brand repetitions before the bond of trust is high enough to generate a transaction. Some trust-building methods may be as simple as repeat visits to your website, regularly scheduled email communications, search engine exposures or targeted ad banner repetition on well-respected websites. The messages to reinforce through your communications could include:

- ✓ Superior customer service (Nordstrom's)

- ✓ Reliability – spend more now and save money over the long haul (John Deere)

✓ Exceptional Quality or Image (Prada, Gucci, Estée Lauder, Armani, Calvin Klein)

Conversion Marketing

Now, with an understanding of the online marketing fundamentals, we can start our exploration of Conversion Marketing. Once someone starts interacting with your products/services, your opportunity to close the sale is within your grasp. Remember that your eCommerce conversion rates are the key to success. To calculate the ratio of Visitors to Buyers, divide the number of visitors to your site by the number of transactions to get your Conversion rate, as shown below:

Visitors:	**3,400**
Transactions:	**÷ 68**
Conversion Rate:	**2%**

Measuring this ratio regularly and tracking your promotional activities are the fundamental building block of your success as a Conversion Marketer.

For a copy of the conversion tracking tool used with my consulting clients, visit the URL below to download an Excel document designed to capture conversion data in an organized fashion.

http://www.conversionmarketingbook.com/resources.html

Abandonment Rate:

Have you ever watched someone standing in a long line at the grocery store? Picture the well-dressed young man I saw last week walk up to the Express Line with his three items — a bunch of bananas, a jar of chocolate sauce, and a half-gallon of Rocky Road ice cream. He's juggling his load because he didn't think to grab a hand cart, but he's sure the line's going to be quick. Five minutes later, his line hasn't budged.

The freezing cold ice cream carton is making his hands tingle as he shifts it from one hand to the other. A banana falls off the bunch and lands on the floor. The grumbling starts, the sighing, the craning of the neck, looking for the obstruction at the front of the line. "What is the hold up? I mean, I've just got a few — >>CRASH<<! There goes the jar of chocolate sauce, splattering all over the floor. He looks around, wide-eyed and mouth open, everyone staring at him. What do you think he'll do next? He'll head for the nearest exit as fast as possible! He's embarrassed about the scene he caused, mad about the slow checkout lane and is disappointed that he didn't get to enjoy his dessert. This is an illustration of "Shopping Cart Abandonment", where shoppers enter your Shopping Cart and leave without making a purchase.

Minimizing the number of clicks between the product pages and checkout in your ecommerce catalog is as important as a fast checkout line at the grocery store.

Minimizing the number of clicks between the product pages and checkout in your ecommerce catalog is as important as a fast checkout line at the grocery store. The standard rule of thumb is to expect a 50% drop-off rate each time a Buyer is required to view an additional page while checking out of your shopping cart. The Abandonment Rate is the rate at which people leave your website in the middle of the transaction. Experienced Conversion Marketers will track the Abandonment Rate of their shopping cart and work to minimize the number of clicks in the checkout process. To illustrate how, let's run some math.

Suppose it costs roughly $2.00 to get a Visitor to your website. This number factors in all the costs associated with driving traffic — your time, design costs, advertising, promotion, and anything else related to bringing people to your site. Let's assume you have twelve Visitors who come to your site. If you have two clicks between your product landing page and your checkout, and there's a 50% drop-out rate between each click, then six of twelve visitors will drop out on the first click, while three of the remaining six will drop out on click number two. This leaves three buyers prior to the entering of payment information. The true cost per Visitor is $8.00, as 75% of interested buyers were lost in the checkout

23

process if your Shopping Cart requires 2 clicks from product to order completion.

Illustration of Minimizing Clicks to Checkout

STEPS	2 CLICKS TO CHECKOUT	1 CLICK TO CHECKOUT
Number of Visitors	12 👥👥👥👥👥👥	12 👥👥👥👥👥👥
Clicks to Checkout	🖱️🖱️	🖱️
Visitors Dropped on Click 1	👥👥👥👥👥👥	👥👥👥👥👥👥
Visitors Dropped on Click 2	👥👥👥	Ø
Cost/Acquisition	$8.00	$4.00

This illustration assumes the cost per Visitor is $2.00

When you are able to reduce the number of clicks in your Shopping Cart from 2 to 1 clicks, then the Cost per Buyer drops to $4.00, dramatically reducing your acquisition costs.

THE CONVERSION LOOP
THE SIMPLICITY OF
AUTOMATION

Now that we've covered the fundamentals on how to think about the online economy and how goods are promoted online, let's explore converting visitors into buyers, in terms of the Conversions Loop methodology. To illustrate the conversions process, let's take a look at conversions in terms of planning a glamorous party hosted to raise investment for a start-up company.

CELEBRATE

Let's say you wanted to throw a party. The process of bringing people together for a celebration is a lot like the process of bringing traffic to your website and converting those casual visitors into customers – what we call the Conversion Loop. Whether we're talking about a dinner party for a few friends or a grand fund-raising dinner, both involve a four-step process to bring people closer and closer to the goal you have in mind.

An ophthalmologist friend of mine organized an informal gathering at his home to tell his friends about an opportunity to invest in a technology start-up for doctors. Guests were greeted at the door of his elegant waterfront home by a Spanish guitarist to set the mood. A serving staff was busy in the kitchen, rolling-out a tantalizing stream of gourmet appetizers to accompany the fine wine served to guests. Mid-party, a group of executives gave an overview of the investment opportunity in the company, accompanied by the "call-to-action" of reviewing an investment prospectus. The process of putting together this fund-raiser party is no different than operating a Conversion Marketing campaign. A four-step formula for guiding people through a buying decision closely aligns with the process of planning a party. When it all comes together, everybody wins.

Step 1) The first thing to do when you throw a party is decide whom you want to come and send invitations. This is similar to identifying the Target audience for your marketing campaigns.

Step 2) Once you send out your invitations, the next step is to see who is interested and get their RSVP.

Step 3) As the date gets closer, you remind the people on your guest list how great your event will be, communicate directions and confirm that they'll be there.

Step 4) Finally the day arrives and so do the folks you invited. Open the door and let them in. That list of people you started out with is converted into a roomful of guests, and everyone has a great time!

Here's how that process looks in the online world, using the Conversion Loop method.

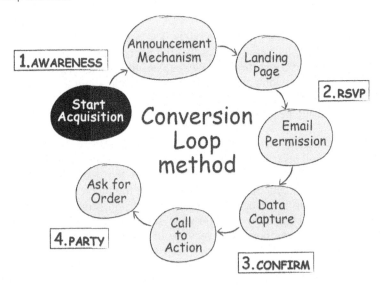

Conversion Loop Step 1 – Invitation

In the Conversion process, your Announcement Mechanism is like your party invitation. You have to decide on the type of people you want to attract to your website and speak to them in a way that gets their attention. You have to create interest. We live in an age of information overload, and never before have peoples' lives been so hectic and complex.

Your invitation has to reach out to the people you care about, and it must uniquely capture their attention above the din of all the other things going on in their busy lives. This is true with your Announcement Mechanism as well.

In order to let people know about your goods and bring traffic to your site, you've got to let people know you have what they need. You have to excite their desire for your product. Here is a resource of 9 methods to create AWARENESS for your website:

1. **Website Content –** having a compelling and attractive website is a great way to attract visitors. Use of free content, relevant information, articles or great prices are excellent methods of attracting Visitors to your website. We will cover a few more ideas in Chapter 7.

2. **Search Engine marketing strategy** - this method can produce massive traffic if you are able to use keyword phrases that get your website listed in the top 10-20 listings on major search engines. Historically, the largest and most significant search engine in terms of traffic is Google, but this trend changes rapidly with the onset of hungry competitors. Also be on the lookout for search engines that are relevant to your industry as these may be more conducive to your success. Getting top placement of a certain keyword phrase is often quite difficult with keywords commonly searched like "real estate" or "new cars". Massive traffic waits when you use keyword terms with low competition. What makes a website rank high in search listings tends to change dramatically month to month based on how the search engines determine which websites are relevant.

When I work with companies on website traffic, a keyword study is conducted called a Blue Ocean Index Study. This term was inspired by the book *Blue Ocean Strategy* which explores companies with business models designed to circumvent highly competitive marketplaces and establishing a beachhead in uncontested waters. When running a Blue Ocean Index Study, we look for unique and clever high-traffic keyword phrases that are currently being searched online, which have relatively low competition. CASE STUDY: A first-time author I work with, Dawn Jones, achieved the #1 Best Seller position on iTunes for her audiobook using this simple method for getting traffic using this keyword optimized title: The Top 7 Personality Challenges.

3. Public Relations - Public Relations is typically in the form of a newsworthy press release published on your website and posted to news outlets. Pubic Relations, often called PR, can be a very economical form of driving traffic, especially if your release is picked-up by a major news outlet, journal or magazine. A good press release will be timely, newsworthy and will contain links back to your website for more information. Publishers daily pick-up relevant press releases with breaking news on an industry and provide valuable exposure and traffic to your website.

One success story is from a professional speaker named Keith Harrell, who had an extraordinary PR experience. One day, Keith was contacted by a reporter writing a story on "A Day in the Life" of a professional speaker. The reporter contacted six speakers with a request to be interviewed. Keith was the only speaker who responded to her call, therefore the reporter ran a full-page article featuring one speaker, Keith Harrell. As it turns out, the reporter was working on this article for the Wall Street Journal. Through this one event, this speaker went from virtual obscurity to fame overnight, which led to his success with a New York Times best selling book and a multi-million dollar speaking business.

4. Media - Buying targeted media is an efficient method to drive traffic to your website, and is very popular with marketers. The key to large scale media buying is managing efficiencies. To make media buying profitable requires an excellent Branding strategy, great creative and a well thought through Conversion strategy. There are many forms of media including television, outdoor, print and paid placement. A few popular forms of online media are illustrated below, which often can be targeted effectively and measured efficiently:

Pay Per Click (PPC) Advertising – A company called Overture, which was purchased by Yahoo!, pioneered the PPC business. Companies like Google and Facebook have dominated this industry with their advertising inventory which allows amazing audience targeting capabilities. These advertising tools are helpful to small business and mega-advertisers alike. A pay-per-click ad only costs the advertiser when an individual clicks the ad and visits the advertiser's website. It is a very efficient form of advertising because you only pay for people interested enough to click on your advertisement. The commercialization of this form of advertising has revolutionized the advertising industry as we know it, since even small advertisers can reach a global audience with their advertisements.

Ad Banners – online advertising started with the simple ad banner, which appears on webpages typically with animated graphics. Ad banners are traditionally sold on a Cost Per Thousand basis (which the industry refers to as CPM). Advertisers pay for the ads whether a consumer clicks on the banner or not.

Email List Rental – web publishers are skilled at getting people to opt-in to receive email. Publishers will rent-out their lists to advertisers who can send advertisements to subscribers in the form of a solo email or a newsletter ad.

Co-registration – Email publishers will promote an incentive to people in exchange for signing-up for various email newsletters. The email list publisher benefits by grouping their offer to join a newsletter with other newsletter publishers, as the costs to attract Visitors is shared among several advertisers. Incentives typically offered by co-registration companies include free downloads, sweepstakes or valuable information. The quality of email lists created by co-registration marketing can be a bit suspect as the people signing up are primarily motivated by free goods or a chance to win a big prize which often can be completely unrelated to your product/service.

5. Incentive Offers - Luring Visitors to your website with a compelling and targeted incentive is a proven method for attracting traffic to your website. The more targeted your incentive, the more targeted your traffic. The incentive serves the dual purpose of also capturing information in exchange for the incentive. When planning incentive offers for a marketing campaign, spend time picking the perfect incentive to stimulate desire with your audience versus a need. An example of a targeted incentive is giving away a popular video game when seeking a target audience of young males 18-25 years old. The young man may need a tank of gas, but he desires the value of the entertainment experience.

6. Social media sites – User generated content has taken the web by storm. Several significant historical events in the social media scene include News Corp's $580 million purchase of MySpace.com, Google's $1.6 billion purchase of YouTube.com and Facebook's multi-billion dollar IPO (Initial Public Offering). Social media sites enable consumers to publish personal information and build communities around special interests. A few interesting companies in the social media space include Facebook, Linked In, Twitter and YouTube. Marketers can take advantage of social media trends by getting involved in relevant ways with your audience. To see how talented marketers are using social media, spend some time looking at how big marketing companies like Nike and Coca-Cola are using this form of media.

7. Blogs – coming from the term web log, a blog is a website published using easy self-service tools featuring text, graphics and videos on subject-matter important to the blog creator. Blogs typically include short commentary or news on a particular subject and are extremely important in engaging your audience. Blogging is also a great method to generate traffic from search engines.

8. Offline Marketing – an economical and often overlooked method of driving traffic to a website is publishing your website address in strategic locations offline. Traditional retailers have a strong advantage in converting store traffic into online traffic via signage, register receipts and shopping bags. Where can you publish your website to drive traffic offline to online?

9.   Word of Mouth – referrals from friends, colleagues and relatives serve as the single, most-influential source of traffic to a website. Some marketers call this "Viral Marketing" as the word about your website can spread like a virus. This is a good thing! Respected referrals are the most effective method of driving sales conversions.

Conversion Loop Step 2 – RSVP

Once visitors become aware of what you do and the goods you offer on your site, you can confirm their desire – or get their RSVP. In the Conversion Loop, this is called Data Capture and Permission to Engage. People who opt-in to get email from your company have elected to receive information from your company.

Getting email permissions or Fans/Follows/Likes is key.

In Conversion Marketing, we call these people Interested Visitors. This process weeds out those who aren't interested or aren't able to come to the party. It gives you a pool of resources to work with and a way to maximize your focus. It gives you an audience to tell your story to.

Once you've acquired Permission to Engage, you'll need to apply certain techniques when collecting your visitors' data. You want to ask your visitors for enough information to target your marketing, but not so much that it intimidates them.

> "Data acquisition increases only up to a point."

People are often glad to give you their first name and email address. Asking for personal or lifestyle information can sometimes have the opposite effect of what you want to achieve. When the questions you're asking become too invasive, participation drops off, and there's a sharp decline in traffic. By asking non-personal questions, you can get more data from Visitors and a stronger likelihood that they'll come back to you. Here are a few questions that are okay to ask in an online survey:

✓ First Name

✓ Email address

✓ Zip code

✓ Gender

✓ Preference questions, such as likes and dislikes.

Once you've captured data from your Visitors, you can segment your email list into groups, enabling you to send the most pertinent information possible to the interests of each group. For instance, if you operate a sporting goods store, you may not want to send weight lifting product offers to the golfers in your email database. The goal is to maximize the rate that your emails are opened to get return visits to your website. Targeting your audience with relevant information or product offerings will move people to pay attention to your messages.

Conversion Loop Step 3 – Confirmation

You've attracted people to your website. You've narrowed down your prospects to include only Interested Visitors, and you have their permission to engage. Next comes the engagement, or confirmation. In the Conversion Loop, it's called Repetition. Less than two percent of first-time visitors purchase on the first visit to an unfamiliar website.

> *Less than 2% of first-time visitors purchase on the first visit to an unfamiliar website.*

Establishing a bond of trust takes Repetition or a series of repeated exposures to your messages, brand or products. Your Interested Visitors have to get used to the idea of owning your product. It has to become comfortable. In fact, it has to be downright cozy before they'll part with their hard-earned cash. Traditional branding studies show that it takes several branding exposures to achieve trust. This means that in order to trust you enough to buy from your company, your Interested Visitors must have repeated exposures to your message to build that relationship. Odds are they won't do purchase on their own. You need to confirm with your visitors, using repetition, to stimulate purchase intent. You need to engage them again and again.

You have their permission and your audience wants to hear from you – they gave it to you back in Step 2. If you invest the effort in your Interested Visitors, they become repeat visitors to your website through the Repetition process. That means the two of you get acquainted, and they get comfortable with the idea of owning your goods (or coming to your party).

Here are some effective tools used in the Repetition process to create a positive response from your Interested Visitors and convert them into customers.

- ✓ Email newsletter with reminders of who you are

- ✓ Social Media messages keep your message in front of consumers

- ✓ Special offers to entice repeat visits

- ✓ Compelling content relevant to their lifestyle or profession. Consider using articles, industry research, videos or audios recordings.

Only a few people will buy the first time they visit a website – but they do buy! One key to creating a profitable website is to create an emotional attachment or a relationship with your company. Have you ever tried to create an emotional response from someone when face-to-face? What kind of things would you do to create an emotional response? Creating an emotional attachment can be a challenge face-to-face but how can you create emotion, like excitement or fear, in an impersonal online environment? Let's explore 3 ideas used to create DESIRE online.

1. Emotional attachment

Testimonials – show pictures and statements from people who are delighted customers. People will gravitate to images or titles of people to whom they feel they can relate. Use imagery of people representative of your target audience who have had a need fulfilled by your product or service.

Security – you can help people feel rest assured with their purchase decision by providing these assurances:

- ✓ 100% satisfaction guarantee

- ✓ Money-back policy

- ✓ 30-day return policy, no questions asked

Credit card logos – surprising studies have proven that products sell 25% more, in terms of the dollar value, when a credit-card logo is displayed near the point of purchase. People understand that if they're not satisfied, they can use their credit-card issuer as leverage to get purchases refunded which do not meet expectations.

2. Relevance

Your website can be equipped with simple, yet effective tools which help your Visitors to see your product in a relevant situation:

- ✓ Les Schwab features a tool on their website which allows visitors to see the make/model of your vehicle with a new set of high-margin chrome rims.

- ✓ Clothing or cosmetics matched with the visitor's color palette are offered by various department stores. An example is a woman with autumn skin and hair coloring can expect to see good results with certain cosmetics and clothing choices.

✓ Video of your product in-use can be very effective. I recently viewed an effective use of video from a manufacture of locking mailboxes. The video shows a hard-working identity thief, struggling to unsuccessfully pry open a secure-locking mailbox with a crowbar.

These are excellent methods of driving conversion by stimulating a relevant experience using tools unique to the Internet.

3. Relationship

Creating rapport and a relationship with your visitors can be achieved using these proven methods:

✓ Capture email addresses and communicate on a regular basis with your Interested Visitors.

✓ In addition to capturing email addresses, capture a small amount of non-personal data so you can send personalized and relevant offers. Capturing this data can be accomplished in online surveys.

✓ Segment your email lists into groupings so you can focus the content of your newsletters to the DESIRES of your audience.

Conversion Loop Step 4 – Let's Party!

Finally the day arrives. The folks you invited/engaged/confirmed have been converted into a roomful of guests. Everyone is having a great time at your swanky soirée. It's the same experience with your Interested Visitors on your website. If you've successfully handled the first three steps in a methodical fashion, Conversion falls into place naturally. Through your Announcement Mechanism, potential buyers became interested. By getting their Permission to Engage, they establish a relationship with you. Through tempting offers and repetition, their interest is ignited into desire. Voila! Your visitors have been converted to Customers.

Here are 8 powerful techniques that move the conversion process to completion:

1. Limited time offers - This is a proven conversion tactic to create the motivation to buy today. If you put a time limit on the availability of your product, it creates fear of loss. Take a page from the eBay playbook where products have a fixed time limit before the deal is gone for good. The fear of loss is often a more powerful purchase incentive than the positive benefit of ownership.

> *The fear of loss is often a more powerful purchase incentive than the positive benefit of ownership.*

2. Trial close – Trial closes are techniques used worldwide by highly-paid sales executives. A trial close could come in the form of a question, such as "Do you like the blue model, or is the red model more suited to your taste?"

Here are a series of trial close tools that can be deployed online to transform an Interested Visitor into a customer.

a) Free trial offers – offer a limited-time, free trial of your product to move Interested Visitors closer to a buying decision. This is used widely with subscription services or consumable products (i.e. one-month-free trial).

b) Low-cost trial – many highly successful direct marketers will offer a $.01 trial offer in exchange for a product worth $10-$20 in order to establish a buying relationship. The benefit of this method is important in subscription-based pricing models, where the $.01 also verifies that the consumer has a valid credit-card. Subscription services have been using this method successfully for decades in the music and book publishing industry.

3. Gift with purchase – this is an especially effective psychological tool to use. Information marketers will offer hundreds of dollars in downloadable incentives with the purchase of a book. Business-to-business marketers also use this effectively, especially when they cater the free gift to the personal desires of their clients such as a golf outing or fishing trip.

4.   Discounts – a discount offer pretty much speaks for itself. However, all discount offers are not created equal! Often, the manner in which you communicate your discount can have a dramatic impact on response rates. Here is a hierarchy of the top-performing discount offers, listed in terms of effectiveness. Make a copy of this chart and put it near your desk.

   a)   Free – this is the most powerful word in the English language and is proven to motivate people into action.

   b)   50% Off – If the margin structure of your product/service supports a 50% discount structure, this offer can generate a flurry of orders.

   c)   Buy One, Get One Free – this technique is popular with consumable products which are purchased often.

   d)   Buy One, Get One Half Off – consider using this offer with higher priced merchandise or services.

   e)   Buy Two, Get One Free – if you are seeking to increase market share, this can be effective in thwarting competitive purchases for a period of time.

   f)   Coupon offers – coupons with a cash savings which are discounted at the time of purchase. The higher the value of your coupon determines the percentage redemption rate.

   g)   Mail-in Rebates – always communicate your rebates in terms rounded up to the full dollar amount (i.e. $10.00 off performs better than $9.97 off). Marketers can often promote a higher dollar value of a rebate than a coupon, as redemption rates of Rebates are often lower than Coupons due to the drop-off rates associated with extra steps required to mail-in a rebate offer.

Which of these discount offers, listed in order of response rates, are relevant to your products or services? Check the ones which apply or create your own ranking.

DISCOUNT OFFER Ranking Chart

5. Free shipping - Some products purchased online are perceived by consumers as more expensive because of shipping costs. Free or very low cost shipping is proven to be quite reliable in bridging this gap in the mind of consumers.

6. Customer Service - Highly responsive customer service creates value in any buying situation. If you can offer a toll-free number with a live person answering the phone, you'll be way ahead of your competition. Other automated methods of exceptional customer service can include

a) Timely email follow-up. Younger generations feel that a 5-minute response to email inquiries is long.

b) Alternate Ordering – order by phone or fax ordering options are relevant for certain industries (like business to business) or mature customers.

7. Selection - Everyone loves options. Choice gives your consumer a feeling of empowerment. Too much choice, though, and customers may become victims of "analysis paralysis." After all, who can make up their mind when presented with fifteen shades of blue from which to choose? Customers typically follow the path of least resistance. Too much choice can become an obstacle to purchasing. Not enough choice will cause your Interested Visitor to move on. Find the right balance for your business.

8. Free Installation - Free installation service are an effective marketing tool for technical products sold to a non-technical audience. This is great for items such as cable TV, expensive televisions, Internet services, office equipment, phone systems, and other common technical goods and services.

The magic behind driving sales conversions online is moving Interested Visitors from the "fact-finding mode" to the "Gotta Have It! mode."

Online conversion can sometimes be tricky for some products/services because the Interested Visitor can't touch or feel your product. Here's an example of how one successful vendor achieved success despite this challenge.

In my travels to a speaking engagement, I had the chance to meet a woman working on her eCommerce company on the plane. Her name was Mary and I gathered that her life situation wasn't all that glamorous. She lived in a tiny home in a tiny town in the desert east of Los Angeles with less than 10,000 people, without a lot of opportunity. In fact she was cleaning houses and taking on odd jobs to make ends meet. Yet she had an uncommon attitude, and she decided that she was going to go into business for herself. She made a few false starts and didn't seem to be getting any traction in her financial life.

One day Mary discovered an unusual opportunity to buy discounted inventory of Thomas Guide maps, back when people used printed maps to navigate around town. Now, these were maps that you can buy at any variety store, bookshop or grocery outlet. They were a commodity item. Mary had a tough time selling them door-to-door in her spare time. Her market was small and she quickly exhausted all her prospects. But she had an investment inventory to sell. So, Mary decided to create a website and market the Thomas Guide map books online.

On her first attempt, Mary's inventory didn't sell. With so many other companies offering the same product, her little mom-and-pop operation in the desert hardly got noticed. But Mary persistently kept at it, and eventually she came to understand the principles of Conversion Marketing.

- ✓ She decided who her best prospects were.

- ✓ She learned how to get noticed on search engines.

- ✓ She captured information on her leads

- ✓ She created an opportunity for repeat exposures.

- ✓ Using Conversion tools such as free shipping and great customer service, she soon had more customers than she could handle.

Not only did she run out of her initial stock, but Mary was soon utilizing drop shipping and other mass-marketing principles of Internet Conversion Marketing. Mary was able to turn her circumstance into a six-figure income, and take her family on vacations while still living in that tiny desert town east of Los Angeles. Mary met her goals, and her lifestyle took a turn for the better.

That brings us to our next chapter on the importance of knowing where you're headed. Let's talk about your sales conversion targets and working toward your goals.

THE MAGICAL POWER OF INTENTION

As you will discover in more depth in the upcoming chapter on the Psychology of Conversion, there is proven power, measured by behavioral psychologists, in making written declarations of your intentions which I call the Power of Intention. With few exceptions, the excellent salespeople and marketers with whom I have worked have applied the Power of Intention to their professional lives. It is a common denominator that separates excellent results from good results.

Statistics show that by simply reading this book, an act of actively investing in your professional development, you are in the top 10% of marketing and business professionals. Putting the Power of Intention to work, as illustrated in this chapter, will propel you into the top 3% of marketers worldwide. How does the Power of Intention work?

Something powerful happens when you set a goal, when you identify the direction you're heading, and the path you will take to get there. As you think things through, you become clear about the direction you're heading. It becomes obvious what will help you achieve your objective, and what activities are distractions. As a result, you spend more time focusing on the things that really matter. I've seen this accomplished with speakers, authors, musicians, entrepreneurs, amateur athletes and successful business executives. This is true in many aspects of a successful life, and plotting your Conversion Marketing goals is no exception, which is why helpful tools are provided in this book.

Having clearly defined goals up front is essential in the design of your Conversion Marketing strategy. This chapter describes how to structure an exceptional Conversion Marketing strategy by creating measurable goals, establishing a realistic budget, and creating a timeline for achieving those goals. Spreadsheets and resources are included to help speed up the process rather than "reinventing the wheel."

I worked with a young woman named Meagan, who came from a fairly ordinary background. Though she'd made good grades in school, Meagan did not have superior intelligence. She was middle-class, and like most people, she had never owned her own business. In fact, she'd been passed over for promotions twice at the company where she worked as an Affiliate Marketing Manager. She seemed to be drifting along in life, doing alright but not getting ahead, not claiming her share of career advancement opportunities that seemed to come so easily to other people.

One day Meagan met an exciting man – very wealthy – a man she really admired and with whom she connected. He was personally successful in his business, but it also seemed that he had tapped into some secret that created an irresistible magnetism for him. He had the Midas Touch in all areas of his life. The two began dating and enjoyed a romantic lifestyle, which I witnessed from afar. After a time, they got married.

What Meagan learned about him is that he used the power of goal setting to create the life he desired. He knew what he wanted, committed his goals to paper and then went after those goals. That's when the light turned on for Meagan. Her husband modeled for her the key to career success that she'd been missing. She made a decision early in their marriage to tap into the same success by declaring her own goals. Soon, Meagan knew she possessed the keys to make it on her own as an entrepreneur.

Meagan set her goals and went to work. She'd always been passionate about becoming an independent meeting planner, so she launched her own business with money she'd saved over the previous years. Blending her panache for decorating and party planning, she created a business plan and got a small-business loan from her bank. Her business involved coordinating with corporate executives, booking five-star venues in exotic locations, hiring entertainers, and sampling gourmet food to build a unique experience for her clients. She had deadlines and commitments, balance sheets and projections. She definitely met challenges along the way, and yet her determination to reach her goals sustained her through the peaks and valleys of running a business. She was committed to her own success like never before.

It took hard work, discipline and a refusal to give-up when hitting roadblocks which every business person encounters. But within two years, Meagan was netting a handsome annual income from her meeting planning company. Meagan travels to exotic resorts worldwide to manage meetings for executive retreats and sales conferences. Her commitment to customer service has earned her an enviable network of referrals. She definitely proved she could hold her own in the realm of business. Today, she and her husband enjoy a doubly opulent lifestyle.

The steps that Meagan took to realize her dream are the same steps involved in achieving any goal. Every meaningful goal in life needs 5 essential components:

1. Be written

When you write a goal, it becomes tangible. It's something you can mail or hand to another person. It's a piece of physical property that you can move. Never underestimate the power of a written declaration.

2. Be specific

Think through the small details. Be clear about the results you're seeking and visualize the outcome.

3. Be measurable

Create quantifiable goals that are easily tracked.

4. Be attainable

Create a vision that you can see yourself achieving. Wrap your mind around your goal. Believe it! If your goal is too big for you to believe right now, create smaller sub-goals. These incremental goals will move you closer to your outcome, generate an upward spiral of confidence as well as the all-important sense of achievement that each of us desire in our hearts.

5. Be attached to a Timeline

Using a timeline is key to evaluate your success. Setting your goals too high and making them unachievable leads to frustration. Don't be hard on yourself. Setting your conversion goals too low can lead to lack of motivation. Go ahead – stretch a little. Success lies just outside of your comfort zone!

> *Value of Goals: 1) Any goal-setting system is better than no system at all; 2) Any plan is better than no plan.*

What Meagan learned is this: 1) Any goal-setting system is better than no system at all; 2) Any plan is better than no plan. The simplest of all principles are the truest – we function best on simple ideas.

The Power of Intention is organized into 14 powerful factors through which to filter your professional goals. By internalizing these factors, you can achieve almost anything!

1. DESIRE

Desire is the only real limitation to your success in building world-class Conversion Marketing campaigns. If you want anything badly enough, you can achieve it. But that's the key: You have to want it. Complacency is your adversary, and there is no success in your comfort zone.

Your goal has to be personal. You can't want a goal for someone else. You can't look to your boss for an increase in pay. You have to earn it, and focusing on your goals will help you produce the rewards you deserve.

In pursuing your goals you will need to create an intense, passionate, burning desire within yourself. When you have a major goal, it's something you don't have to inspire yourself to do. **It's something you must do.** If you're working on your major goal, you become impatient with everything that distracts you from it, and you structure your time to minimize those distractions. Keep you goals where you can see them.

2. BELIEF

Have an absolute conviction that your goal is possible, and know that it's possible for you. Be crystal clear, carry an attitude of certainty. You get results according to your beliefs, and you can tell what your beliefs are by digging deep and looking at your internal convictions. If you don't know what your beliefs are, take a look at your results.

The funny thing is, you don't have to start out with belief. You can start by checking sub-goals off your list, and those actions will create belief. Once you start to carry the posture of belief, you will live into it. Zig Ziglar said, "What you get by achieving your goals is not as important as what you become by achieving your goals."

> "What you get by achieving your goals is not as important as what you become by achieving your goals." Zig Ziglar

3. YOUR "WHY"

Determine all the reasons you want to achieve your goal, and trust that there will come a time for you to be tested. It's just the nature of things. Yet those who risk everything will hang in there and achieve what they set out to do. The more reasons you have for achieving your goals, the more you will become a force of nature. If you have hundreds of reasons for reaching your goals, you will be irrepressible.

4. YOUR STARTING POINT

Be honest - what's the reality of your position? If you want to triple the number of subscribers in your email list, you have to examine your outbound marketing activities and partnerships to determine how far you have to go. Make an honest assessment of where you are today, then recognize the steps you need to take to achieve your goal.

5. MAKE A PLAN

> *Only 3% of Americans have written goals, and the other 97% work for those people.*

Only 3% of Americans have written goals, and the other 97% work for those people. As you develop your marketing strategy, the first thing you have to do is write a Marketing Plan. It clarifies things, forces you to think through every part of the business before you take action.

Make a list everything you need to achieve your goal – a list of what you want, when you want it, and why you want it. Take stock of your obstacles. Identify the people who can help you, along with the information and skills you'll have to get on your own. Decide what you're going to pursue first, then go after each item, step by step.

6. DEADLINE

What is a goal without a deadline? It is just a dream. Our subconscious mind acts according to the deadlines you set. If we don't have a deadline, we naturally tend to procrastinate.

Recognize that the deadline is merely a target enabling you to focus on your project. More importantly, filter out activity unrelated to achieving your goals. It's commonly known that 80% of the work gets done in the final 20% of the budgeted time. Don't abandon your goal if the deadline slips. Merely set a new deadline using the 80/20 Rule. Use deadlines to your advantage!

7. ROADBLOCKS

Identify the obstacles, or roadblocks, you'll have to overcome. Recognize that there's always an obstacle. There's nothing wrong with roadblocks, but be clear about overcoming them when you encounter them.

Also recognize that 80% of your obstacles are internal. If you're not achieving your goals, it's not because of lack of opportunity. We've already demonstrated that Internet Marketing provides a wealth of opportunity and career advancement. Identify the obstacles that originate within you and dig-deep to overcome them using this 14-step process for achieving goals.

What's the one major thing that's preventing you from achieving your goal? If you don't know what it is, become still and look within, or ask trusted friends and colleagues. They'll be sure to tell you! Once you've identified your obstacle and a way to remove it, your path is almost clear.

8. KNOWLEDGE & SKILL

Identify the additional knowledge and skill you need to achieve your conversion goals. What's the one skill that would have the greatest positive impact on your career? Is it search-engine-optimization skills? Copywriting skills? Landing page optimization? Viral marketing implementation? Design and layout skills? Public speaking and/or communication skills? Leadership and management skills? Skills of persuasion? You probably already know the answer – it's the thing you don't like to do or are afraid of doing, that something outside of your comfort zone, the one thing that could utilize all of your other talents.

Take a good look. How can you gain the knowledge and skill you need to push through this resistance? It may be tough to push through your resistance, but positive change always produces a positive result. Look at the rewards you stand to reap!

9. MASTER MIND GROUP

No one achieves greatness alone. It's been said that two minds together create a third, more powerful mind. This is synergy. So it's up to you to identify the people, groups and organizations that can help you succeed. Who can help you the most? What's in it for them? How can you deserve their support? There needs to be an exchange, so spend time creating incentive for people who can mentor you in the skills you need most. Some successful friends of mine are career coaches, which is another avenue to pursue if the idea of having a career "personal trainer" appeals to you.

Conversion Marketing

10. VISUALIZE

Imagine your goal as if it's already a reality. Use affirmations in the present tense. A classic example of positive affirmations is the often repeated statement, "I am the greatest!" from boxing legend Muhammad Ali. Ali's philosophy on life was, "I figured that if I said it enough, I would convince the world that I really was the greatest." See yourself as already having the conditions you desire. Be aware of the emotions you'll feel when you have accomplished what you set out to do, and bask in them day by day. You'll be surprised by how quickly you bring your goal into being.

11. BECOME RELENTLESS

Be persistent and determined to reach your goals. Recognize that the only way to fail... is to quit. So many people quit before they try to achieve their goals and untold dreams fall by the wayside. Recognize that when you fail, you've merely identified one more way not to reach your goal. Henry Ford filed bankruptcy seven times before developing the assembly line for the Model T. Your persistence is the measure of your belief in yourself.

Every act of persistence strengthens you and creates habits of success that build self-esteem. There are no real limits to what you can accomplish except the limits you place on yourself. So how do you become unstoppable? By refusing to stop! Confidently expect to succeed, and you will.

12. OBJECTIVES

Clearly understand your objectives before designing your campaign. So many objectives in Conversion Marketing go far beyond achieving sales revenues. Think of elements such as job satisfaction, job security, creating new jobs, promoting your team members, expanding your mind and serving others. Be clear about what these ideals mean to you personally and pour your passion into your objectives.

13. IMAGINATION

Visit the last pages of this chapter and take a moment right now to write down your highest priority goals. Think about your end-game.

What do you want to achieve in your business? When do you want to achieve it? Why is that important to you? How will you know when you're finished?

Keep in mind that your Conversion Marketing goals will change with time. You may focus your efforts on building your email newsletter for a six-month period then re-channel your marketing dollars to converting newsletter subscribers into customers for another period of time. You can always re-write your goals. Don't get stuck on making it perfect. The important thing is to write your goals.

Now, take advantage of the Power of Intention. It has been proven many times over that people who declare their goals are three-to-ten times as likely to succeed over their non-goal-setting counterparts. Visualize your goals. Project yourself into the future, to a time when you have already achieved your desires. Take some time to enjoy your accomplishments, even before they have become realities. In time, you will live your visualizations. Go ahead – turn to the end of this chapter and start your goal setting today using the template provided.

14. BUDGET

The last step is to set your budget for each established goal. Your goal will be relatively meaningless unless you can assign budget parameters to it. Everyone wants to lower the cost per acquisition, but the reality is that it often requires more dollars spent in strategic areas to achieve Economies of Scale in order to lower the cost per acquisition. Here are some tips to helping establish appropriate budget parameters for your goal-setting activity:

Budgeting Tips for Conversion Marketers

✓ Allocate a percentage of revenues from a previous reporting period.

✓ Create a fixed budget based on marketing expenditures.

✓ Avoid zero-based budgets. These are defined as spending as little as possible to get the maximum result. It's an efficient way to save money, but be cautious of not allocating money to your Conversion Marketing campaign. In extreme cases, you may be saving $25,000 per month on your Conversion Marketing budget but costing yourself $250,000 in lost revenue per month. Look at the total picture.

✓ Your Goals should be measured over a fixed period of time. This provides you the ability to gauge your success and identify opportunities for improvement.

When you get into the habit of writing specific, measurable, attainable, time-specific goals, your whole world will open. You can now confidently step into the life you envision for yourself as a Conversion Marketer. The key is to take time to picture achieving your goals. Tap into the Power of Intention. When you believe it, you'll achieve it!

Sample Conversion Marketing Goals

To "prime the pump" on your Conversion Marketing goals, here are some common Conversion Marketing goals to get started. Take a close look at these goals and modify them for your own purposes. The impact of the small details matters most in the early stages, when you're formulating your strategy. Working toward achieving these goals will likely decrease your cost per action – and that's always a good thing!

✓ Drive incremental product sales over the previous period

✓ Get a chosen number of new subscribers in a given timeframe

✓ Capture a chosen number of sales leads

- ✓ Increase newsletter opt-ins by a specific percentage each month

- ✓ Increase site traffic by an exact number of visitors over the next reporting period

- ✓ Identify a specific number of respondents in a promotional campaign, such as sweepstakes, coupon offer or rebate program

- ✓ Decrease ad banner and pay-per-click (PPC) rates to increase your advertising cost efficiency and lower your cost per acquisition

- ✓ Increase the ratio of unique visitors to buyers by a particular percentage during a given time-frame

- ✓ Increase your repeat-visitor ratio by a respectable percentage over the previous reporting period

- ✓ Increase newsletter click-through rates by a given percentage each month

Put the *Power of Intention* to work.

CAMPAIGN GOAL - SETTING WORKSHEET

YOUR NAME	TODAY'S DATE

CAMPAIGN NAME

DETERMINE YOUR "WHY"

STARTING POINTS FOR YOUR GOAL

1) _____

2) _____

3) _____

BUDGETARY ITEMS	COST
1)	$
2)	$
3)	$

GOAL (Specific, Measurable, Attainable, Realistic, Tangible)	VALUE	TARGET DATE
1)		
2)		
3)		

CAMPAIGN GOAL - SETTING WORKSHEET (Page 2)

SKILLS OR KNOWLEDGE REQUIRED	RESOURCE
1)	
2)	
3)	

POSSIBLE OBSTACLES	POSSIBLE SOLUTIONS
1)	
2)	
3)	

MASTERMIND GROUP	INVITE DATE	CONFIRM DATE
1)		
2)		
3)		
4)		
5)		
6)		
7)		

POST-CAMPAIGN RESULTS

OUTCOMES ACHIEVED	MEASURE
1)	
2)	
3)	

THE CONVERSION MARKETER'S TOOLBOX 24 PROMOTIONAL TOOLS

My inspiration to become an incentive marketing expert came through a friendship with a co-worker named Len. Len and I worked together as sales colleagues at a Fortune 500 corporation in a regional office near San Francisco, just 30 minutes from the Golden Gate Bridge. Len left the corporation we were working for to start his own company, which was a promotions agency supplying premium items to corporate marketing departments. As I dutifully earned my salary, I watched my friend grow his business year after year into a highly profitable, multi-million dollar business.

One event to "push me over the edge" to become an entrepreneur was when I met Len for dinner one night. I chugged-up to a swank restaurant in my lovely (not!) teal-blue four-door company car. As I was getting out of my car, Len pulled up in a fire-engine-red convertible Porsche. By developing an enviable business, Len created an enviable lifestyle for himself and his family.

We decided to take a drive, so I took a deep breath of inspiration and went cornering through the Northern California foothills with the top down. We were laughing about old times and talking through innovative ideas to bring to the world of promotions. Len is what I describe as a promotional genius. When it comes to creative promotional ideas he always comes through with unbelievable ideas, which is precisely why for the last decade I call him first for his services. As we were talking, thoughts started to take shape about how to create a new, never-before-tried business.

Hence, inspired by the innovative discussion, I decided to open a promotional agency. But I wanted to have some kind of advantage over the hundreds of other promotional agencies out there. At the time I was working for an Internet company that was a "Gold Partner" in the launch of Internet Explorer 3.0, meaning our URL was hard-coded into the Browser as a Favorite website. That meant that the company's website was getting LOTS of website traffic. So I wrote-up what I knew about promotional marketing on the Internet into a Business Plan, as young as the commercial Internet was in 1996, and created an online-promotions technology company.

Little did we know that I would be pioneering the definition of "online sweepstakes" and "viral-marketing-incentive campaigns." As a pioneer, I can tell you that traveling the metaphorical dusty trails in a covered wagon is not all that glamorous. Like my great grandparents who pushed west to settle new lands, I discovered that pioneering takes a tremendous amount of work and a high tolerance for risk.

Since these humble beginnings, I've had the opportunity to work with hundreds of interesting business executives in New York City, London, Paris and all the way into the bayous of Louisiana. What you are about to read is a summary of the online Conversion Marketing campaigns that work.

Now to the nitty gritty – let's talk about how to put your promotional goals into action.

As an Internet marketer, you have a dazzling array of tools available to you. Almost too many tools. The trick is to know which tool to use for your desired effect, and when you should put other tools away.

The tools you use for your business will vary depending on your Brand image, the product or service that you offer, and your target-audience profile. Your choice of tools will also depend on your price point, time on the market, as well as the time of year.

Let's take a look at the different types of Conversion Marketing tools and the best use for each tool. You may want to start a profile of your Conversion Marketing goals, as it will help in the decision-making process. Use the form at the end of this chapter to identify tools which are appropriate for your business.

Here is an overview of 24 Conversion Marketing Tools you can start putting into action to generate sales increases on your website.

1. Dramatic Imagery

If your goal is to create a positive impression associated with your brand, then create positive associations when visitors come to your website with rich imagery related to your products and services. A few practitioners of this art include Prada, Gucci and National Geographic. BMW was famous early-on for creating a series of high-quality action videos featuring superstars like Madonna, which were wildly successful in attracting attention.

2. Coupon or Promotional Code

Online, a coupon is usually a promotional code that can be exchanged for a financial discount when purchasing a product. Offline coupons can also be delivered as a printable image from a web page or can be sent via email for offline redemption.

3. Discount

Discounts and allowances are reductions to a basic price, typically communicated as a percentage off the normal price.

4. 2-for-1 Special

For consumer products, this powerful incentive is effective at driving conversions by offering two products for the price of one. For some products, a 2-for-1 offer can far exceed the performance of a 50% off promotion, despite the fact that the net effective discount is similar. You can also use this tactic to stave-off trials of competitive products.

5. Refer-A-Friend Incentive

Knowing that each new visitor to your website has a cost, offering a free gift or incentive to current Visitors who refer friends is an efficient means of lowering your cost-per-visitor ratio.

6. Gift With Qualified Action

A gift with action is a tool used to stimulate a conversion using an incentive bonus. Examples could include giving away an artist's hot new album with the purchase of a phone, or a book with the purchase of an exotic vacation package.

7. Self Liquidator

A mail-in offer for an incentive item typically offered for a nominal shipping & handling fee. Marketers using self-liquidators will offer a highly related incentive item, with a qualified purchase. An example is to give away a popular video game with the purchase of a gaming accessory, like a video console controller. It has been proven effective to charge a minimal shipping and handling fee (i.e. $4.99-$7.99) for high-value premium items.

8. Scavenger Hunt

An old-fashioned scavenger hunt is a fun method of encouraging people to tour your website and learn more about your products/services. Clues or tokens are placed strategically throughout your website to encourage Visitors to explore specific pages. Clues or tokens are viewed or collected by visitors.

When all the clues are collected, they can be exchanged for a certificate, an entry into a Sweepstakes or other incentive. Visitors can find the clues nested throughout your website by using a treasure map, via a questionnaire or by clickable icons.

9. Recommendations Engine

A Recommendations Engine is a system that suggests similar products to website visitors automatically based on previous purchase behavior or products previously viewed in your catalog. This is an automated function based on products tagged with similar attributes or that are highly complimentary. You will see companies making dynamic product recommendations of related products as you put items into your shopping cart. You can see a powerful example of this at Amazon.com, where they display products purchased by previous customers.

10. Rating System

A Rating System enables consumers to rate products purchased. Famous examples include the Netflix movie-rating system and eBay's seller-rating system. This system validates products like few other features, as consumer ratings appear unbiased. In today's marketplace, user-generated content will have a positive impact on your bottom line. This is a powerful form of "social proof," a concept we will explore in coming chapters.

11. Best-Seller Listing

A best-seller list helps consumers quickly browse the most popular items in your catalog. To add credibility to your top-selling products, try adding a best-seller list, either edited weekly or dynamically based on product sales, to your website. A best-seller list also helps people get quickly to your most-popular items.

12. Rebates

A Rebate is where consumers are offered money back when proof-of-purchase is mailed to the manufacturer. This proof-of-purchase includes receipt, the UPC code (barcode) or other proof of sale. Rebate offers are tried-and-true method for generating additional sales.

Conversion Marketing

The beauty of a rebate offer is that it will stimulate a purchase based on the discount offered on the rebate. However the redemption rates will rarely exceed 25%. For example, if you sell an item for $99.00 and offer a $25 mail-in rebate with a 25% redemption rate on 100 purchases, then your effective discount was only 6%, with a perceived value of a 25% discount. Here is how to calculate this rebate offer: 100 purchases x 25% = 25 redemptions. 25 x $25 = $625. Total sales were $99.00 x 100 = $9,900. Redemption % was $625/$9,900 = 6%.

How to Estimate Rebate Redemption

	Example	Enter Your Estimates
Unit Purchases	100	
Rebate Redemption %	25%	
Face Value of Rebate	$25	
Revenue/Sale	$99	
Total Revenue	$9,900	
Quantity of Redemptions	25% x 100 = 25	
Cost of Rebate .	25 x $25 = $625	
Actual Rebate Redemption Ratio	$626 / $9,900 = 6%	

*Actual cost of Rebate may include Clearing House fees on each rebate redeemed, not illustrated here.

However, be careful with rebate offers. One product which I sold chainwide in Costco warehouse clubs had a retail price of $28. When Costco offered a $10 instant rebate at the cash register representing a 35% discount, a 50% redemption rate was realized. This was much higher than we expected and impacted the profitability of this promotional campaign.

13. Free Samples

Free product and service samples are given to consumers to stimulate trial and awareness of your product offerings. Stimulating Trial can be an effective tool for winning market share for new products. In eCommerce, free samples of downloadable products are typically cost effective to deliver.

14. Point of Purchase

Seasonal and promotional graphics posted to your website can be used to communicate relevant products. iTunes does an excellent job of posting relevant promotional messages in a highly dynamic fashion based on your musical tastes and past purchase behavior.

15. Games of Chance

A game of chance is what the industry calls a sweepstakes or instant win game. Typically these campaigns are short-term promotions generating action by enticing consumers to submit their personal information in exchange for a chance to win a prize. These entries into the contest are often tied to products where "bigger-than-life" prizes are given away. Prizes are carefully selected to generate an emotional response with the target audience.

Sweepstakes

A game of chance where the consumer submits personal information in exchange for a random opportunity to win an inspirational prize at the end of a specified timeframe. Sweepstakes are typically 30-60 days in duration. Sweepstakes have proven successful to marketers with data capture goals and product awareness goals.

Instant Win Game

A game of chance where website visitors who participate in the game are randomly selected in real-time as winners in exchange for performing pre-specified actions. Like sweepstakes, Instant Win games are proven successful to marketers with data capture goals and product awareness goals. Instant Win games are also excellent tools to generate incremental page views (especially relevant to online publishers motivated to increase Ad Views).

16. Loss Leader

The price of a popular product is temporarily reduced in order to stimulate other profitable sales. A popular use of a Loss Leader is to draw customers into a store where they are likely to buy other related goods. Online grocery stores are famous for offering a terrific deal on frozen turkeys before the Thanksgiving holiday, knowing that shoppers are likely to purchase stuffing, pies, drinks and other items to accompany their holiday meal.

17. Price-Pack Deal and Bundles

The package price offers a consumer a discount off of a bundle of products, or can provide an extra quantity for the same price (i.e. 50% more). An example of a bundle offer I have commercialized on my website was by combining two related audiobooks bundled together. The product was priced 25% less than the combined MSRP (Manufactures Suggested Retail Price) of the 2 products sold individually. Revenues for this skyrocketed during the holiday season based on the gift giving aspect for 2 gifts from 1 purchase.

18. Loyalty Rewards Program

Loyalty programs, popularized by the airline industry, are an excellent tool for rewarding repeat customers. Consumers collect points, miles or credits for purchases and redeem them for rewards typically selected from a pre-determined catalog of incentive items. Points serve as a form of currency that the Conversion Marketer can use to stimulate repeat purchase behavior. Loyalty programs are typically long-term in nature.

19. Continuity Program

A tool used to reward repeat purchases from your website, such as offering a "Buy 10, Get 1 Free" incentive. Many people can relate to this incentive tactic used by businesses from coffee shops to dry cleaners. Internet marketers use online continuity programs for products that have repeat purchase patterns such as online travel.

20. Gift Card

Various third party vendors can issue gift cards, which can be redeemed on your website using promotional codes. One idea to lower your overall cost per conversion is by giving a gift card away to consumers who enter your sweepstakes.

For example, if your typical cost per first-time conversion is $30 or more and the face value of a free gift card is $10, you can reduce your initial cost per acquisition by two-thirds by giving away $10 gift cards.

Gift cards are a great way to attract new business to your website and are easy to distribute offline at special events and/or trade shows. The more recognizable your brand name, the more effective you will find this tool.

Apple's iTunes division experienced success with this tactic converting new customers in their joint venture partnerships with Pepsi and Starbucks.

21. Deal of the Day

A fresh, new discount or deal offered each day/week can attract repeat visitors to your website. This tool also focuses the Conversion Marketer to think strategically on a daily/weekly basis about products and pricing. Featuring these deals on prominent landing pages will help lead your Interested Visitors into easily finding popular items in your catalog. Mobile app developers love when their apps are featured on Amazon's "Deal of the Day" featured listing, as they have sold hundreds of thousands of units in a single day.

22. Sales Letter

Many small businesses have tremendous success (measured by conversion rates) by creating long sales letters written by professional copywriters, skilled at writing direct response copy. Video-based sales letters are also effective. These sales letters are laden with psychological triggers that influence people to purchase. Sales letters are also created with short copy and a compelling video message.

These sales letters are often very long (20 page documents). Elements of successful sales letters include consumer testimonials, recommendations from authorities; reduce to ridiculous pricing (i.e. for only $.50/day), discounted bundle pricing and more.

I recently attended a class in writing Sales Letters. Part of the requirements of the class was creating a checklist to organize all the elements that go into a successful sales letters. My sales letter checklist of psychological buying triggers currently has 57 items.

23. Customer Testimonial

To generate what marketers call "social proof," customer testimonials are used to build the bond of trust for Visitors. The psychology of word-of-mouth testimonials is a powerful ally for Conversion Marketers with low-brand awareness. An eMarketer survey reveals that an overwhelming 99% of respondents to a recent survey perceive testimonials as "very/somewhat credible."

24. Survey Strategy

I have seen one common thread among the hundreds of professional marketers I have advised. When presented with the opportunity to create a survey to capture data in a contest, almost every marketer uses the contest as an opportunity to conduct market research as a side benefit. The goal to gather market intelligence is noble, because it will help companies better understand their customer. However this can dramatically increase your costs and reduce your promotional results.

One area where I focus like a hawk when advising marketers is the ultimate cost-per-acquisition for each new survey respondent. You can reliably assign a dollar value for each additional question added to the fields of data required to enter a survey. There is a direct cost-per-acquisition consequence for each type of question.

The basic wisdom for running a survey is to require three to five fields of information with seven questions maximum. The consumer VISUALLY perceives a time cost in entering a survey. If the subconscious perception of time of completing an online survey is too great, they'll drop out of the campaign.

Even if you ask questions that are optional or "not required", the visual weight of a survey will impact a Visitors willingness to participate. Also, certain questions create a guaranteed drop-out rate based on the personal nature of the questions.

6 questions to avoid in Conversion Marketing acquisition campaigns:

1. Avoid asking for full name in association with personal financial information (like household income)

2. Avoid asking for full name with questions about children in the household

3. Avoid asking for full mailing address unless you absolutely need this information

4. Avoid asking for a phone number if you can – expect a 50% drop-out rate when this question is asked as consumers strongly resist the idea of getting in-bound telemarketing calls

5. Avoid asking for credit card information. Assume an 80% drop-out rate in non-transactional related surveys.

6. Avoid asking for a Social Security Number – with the increased threat of identity theft, this field of information is unproductive. Assume a 95% drop-off rate with this question. This single question is why the cost per acquisition is relatively high for surveys in industries like online insurance and mortgage loans.

Take a few minutes to jot down some of these ideas that are relevant to your business at the end of this chapter as you start to refine your Conversion Marketing strategy. Having a concise, written summary of relevant ideas will save hours of brainstorming and potentially tens of thousands of marketing dollars from running Conversion Marketing campaigns that are less than perfect.

This Table is a resource to help speed up the decision-making process when deciding which tools to use in upcoming Conversion Marketing campaigns. Take a moment to record which Tools are relevant for your company/product/service and jot down why.

CONVERSION MARKETING TOOLS	RELEVANCE Scale of 1 – 10 (high)
Free Newsletter	
Industry Research Paper	
Sweepstakes	
Instant Win Game	
Scavenger Hunt	
Gift with Qualified Action	
% Discount Offer	
2 For 1 Offer	
Buy 1, Get 1 Free	
Coupon/Promotional Code	
Rebate Offer	
Free Sample	
Free Trial Offer (i.e. subscriptions)	
Loss Leader	
Long Sales Letter (with dozens of Psychological triggers)	
Customer Testimonials	
Deal of the Day	
Celebrity Endorsement	
Authority Endorsement	
Top 10 List	
Limited Quantities	
Loyalty Rewards Program	
Continuity Program	
Bundled Offer or Package Deal	
Visually Stimulating Imagery	
Customer Rating System	
Recommendations Engine	
Refer a Friend	
Self Liquidator	
Seasonal Point of Purchase Graphics	
Gift Card (discount for pre-purchase)	
Unconditional Guarantee	

An additional resource called the Campaign Intake Form is available to download at **www.conversionmarketingbook.com** to help weed through the decision process and focus your time on the perfect promotional tactics for your business.

CLEVER WEBSITE TRAFFIC STRATEGIES

For the last decade I have been helping companies get more traffic to their websites with alluring incentive programs. Have you ever had the problem of getting TOO much traffic to your website? I laugh when I tell this story now, but believe me, I wasn't laughing at the time.

The story unfolds in the early 2000's during the height of the "dotcom boom". At this time, the promotions technology start-up company I founded was acquired by a public advertising company in New York specializing in online advertising. Selling these interactive advertising programs required a strong component of creativity as part of the sales process. The services we sold were relatively expensive. To develop effective marketing campaigns would require a series of executive meetings to plan the campaign execution.

With one client, we closed an up-and-coming technology company with a big online advertising campaign. The campaign design included a complex Instant Win game, coupled with a Viral Marketing supercharger to boost campaign registration.

The client told me he wanted a promotion that was, "Bigger than life, Bryan!" The goal was to obtain a maximum acquisition rate on Visitors during the dates of the promotional campaign. The launch date happened to coincide with the day of the company's IPO (Initial Public Offering) to become a publicly traded company. Needless to say, all eyes were on the website the day of the launch.

So, early one morning my cell phone goes off and gets me out of bed. It's the client!

"Uh oh," I thought, "this can't be good."

It wasn't.

I glanced at my clock and saw that it was 6:30 AM my time, which was 9:30 AM Eastern - the same time as the opening bell on the Wall Street trading floor!

The client informed me that our promotional servers were down and the links to the promotion on his home page were dead. I immediately called our Chief Developer to get him out of bed to fix the problem. Fortunately, we had remote management of the servers in our hosting facility and were able to get the server farm back online quickly.

The promotion was getting so much traffic, that it knocked the servers offline. I laugh about this today as I'd LOVE to have that problem again where too much traffic was hitting my server farm. Having too much traffic is an easy problem to fix. Having not enough traffic to your website can be an expensive problem to fix. Over the years however, I have discovered a few clever techniques to attract sustained traffic to a website without a massive advertising budget.

Two elements contained in this chapter will set you up to be successful in driving traffic to your website: 1) Paid online advertising; and 2) Sources of free traffic. In addition, there are several useful charts that will help in your traffic-planning process.

Paid Advertisements - Get the Word Out!

There are several major forms of paid online advertising, some more effective than others, to advertise on your website. The list of advertising options starts with the ubiquitous banner ad. We will also go in-depth into other online advertising tools, including highly targeted pay-per-click ads, e-mail list rental, co-registration and others. In the section on getting free traffic, you will learn of a few highly effective techniques, closely guarded techniques used by Internet marketing professionals, for getting sustainable volumes of free traffic.

Banner Ads

Ad banners come in various sizes and formats. The Interactive Advertising Bureau publishes a list of standard ad sizes, helping make the job easier for the complex dynamics between the Publishers who run the ads, the advertisers who pay for the ads, and the ad agencies that create the ads. There are terms for various types of banner ads including buttons, interstitials, pop-ups, skyscrapers, webmercials, pre-roll video and more. See the chart for the most commonly used forms of ad banners.

Standard Sizes for Ad Banners & Buttons

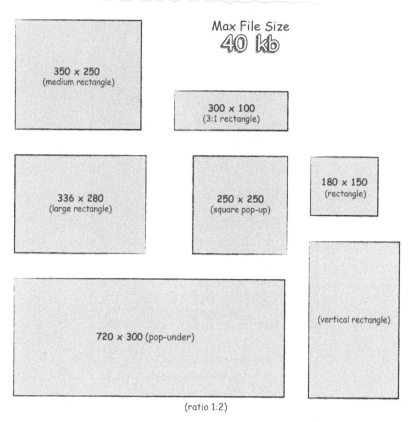

Max File Size
40 kb

350 x 250
(medium rectangle)

300 x 100
(3:1 rectangle)

336 x 280
(large rectangle)

250 x 250
(square pop-up)

180 x 150
(rectangle)

720 x 300 (pop-under)

(vertical rectangle)

(ratio 1:2)

Standard Sizes for Skyscrapers

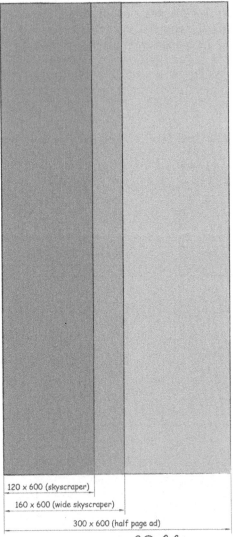

120 x 600 (skyscraper)

160 x 600 (wide skyscraper)

300 x 600 (half page ad)

Max File Size 40 kb

Visit **www.iab.net** for updated information and creative specifications.

Ad banners also come in various technology flavors starting with the basic static banner ad and animated images. Other forms of "rich media" advertising creative technology may include mouse-over features, pull-down menus, predictive ads, dynamically-generated ads and streaming video.

Email List Rental

Similar to direct mail list rental, there are hosts of list brokers who represent Email Publishers who rent their email lists for commercial purposes. To take advantage of list rental, you'll want to locate a vendor within your industry who has the customers you're looking to reach. This topic is covered in more depth in the chapter on email newsletters.

Co-registration

Co-registration websites offer the opportunity to opt-in to multiple email lists on one website. This gives the advertiser the advantage of deferring the costs of driving traffic to the website over multiple advertisers. Co-registration can often be one of the lower cost acquisition techniques, but you may sacrifice quality of leads with some co-registration providers.

Pay Per Click (PPC) Inventory

PPC stands for "pay-per-click" advertising inventory. The Publisher of this form of advertising inventory only gets paid when a consumer clicks upon a display ad. Search engines are by far the most popular source of PPC advertising inventory. Google AdWords, Facebook and Microsoft AdCenter are popular providers of PPC ad inventory. There are also numerous advertising networks who have large inventory of PPC buying opportunities, often with better pricing than the "branded" networks like Facebook and Google.

Free Traffic - 7 Practical Strategies to Increase Traffic

Everyone loves getting free website visitors. The most successful websites have organic traffic that finds them based on reputation, brand or clever website promotion. Let's assume that your website does not have the advantage of huge traffic and that you are seeking lower cost methods to attract visitors to your website. Here are some practical suggestions for getting non-paid traffic to your website.

1. Search Engine Optimization (SEO)

Getting your website listed in the top 10-20 keyword search phrases on Google is probably one of the single best sources of free traffic to your website. This comes as a result having a great website design with properly formatted keyword phrases.

Volumes of books have been written on this subject and the nature of the game changes often. However, for those companies that have figured-out these techniques it is often very profitable. Your success will hinge on which keywords are chosen for optimization. Start thinking of these now, as the keyword phrases for optimization will determine how much traffic you get from search engines.

2. Public Relations

Public Relations, or PR, is an excellent way to spend your time in an effort to attract visitors to your website. There are several large PR services where you can distribute press releases with newsworthy information to reporters worldwide (i.e. PRNewsWire.com, businesswire.com).

In your press releases, include links back to your website to create more traffic and create buzz about your website. Writing articles and distributing them via partner websites and article distribution websites (such as ezinearticles.com) are also excellent sources of free traffic.

3. Referral Marketing

By far, Referral Marketing is the most effective form of advertising. This is when existing members of your community refer their friends to your website. In Marketing classrooms, this phenomenon is also known as "word of mouth advertising."

The reason Referral Marketing is so effective is that when the referral comes from a friend, it comes from someone we know, like and trust. These are the three key ingredients in bonding with people. This philosophy is the cornerstone of the classic book How to Win Friends and Influence People by Dale Carnegie – a great read.

As we established in the chapter on Branding, once the trust is there, making the sale is much easier. Often, the industry refers to online Referral Marketing as Viral Marketing. The first big viral marketing success was the "Blair Witch Project", an independent film that became a huge box-office success off the effectiveness of their ability to spread the word via a clever and mysterious website about the movie.

Viral marketing specialists are seeing excellent success on YouTube. com via short videos. Also, offering your website Visitors an incentive in exchange for referring friends will yield excellent results. Email service providers often include a feature called "Tell A Friend" in each outbound email encouraging your email subscribers the opportunity to refer your website to others.

4. Strategic Partnerships

There are a number of ways that you and a related business can work together to mutually increase your web traffic and your revenue. It's been said that when two minds come together they create a third, more powerful mind – also known as synergy.

> It's been said that when two minds come together they create a third, more powerful mind – also known as synergy.

Aligning your efforts with another company is a great way to leverage time, effort and traffic, and it could even create a built-in system of support. At the same time, you want to make sure you're not so eager for a JV (joint venture) partnership that you engage with just any business. Do your due diligence, and be discerning. Here are great methods for working as a team with another entity. Strategic Partnerships have proven to be one of the most effective methods of promotion for several of my businesses.

- ✓ Email list partnership - You and a joint venture partner form an agreement to promote the other company's promotional offers to your email list(s) in exchange for reciprocal promotion. You send a message to your list in exchange for a partner emailing their list.

- ✓ Reciprocal Linking - Each partner publishes a link to their respective websites, driving cross-traffic among partnering websites.

- ✓ Reciprocal Banner Placement - this is where two websites offer their ad banners to be rotated on websites where there is a decent likelihood of interest in your website.

5. Affiliate Program

I love Affiliate Marketing. The reason is that you don't pay for the traffic to your website unless someone buys something – a true pay-for-performance relationship, much like having dozens of straight-commission salespeople working on your behalf.

Here is how it works. Affiliate Marketing is a system where you pay an Affiliate a commission each time a qualifying action is performed on your website. Qualifying actions can include a purchase (you pay a percentage of the sale) or an email opt-in (you pay a bounty to the affiliate for providing an email subscriber). The Affiliate tracking technology can be part of your eCommerce Shopping Cart system, it can be custom built by your website developers or it can be licensed from several providers which you can find by searching "affiliate tracking technology" on your favorite search engine.

Affiliate Networks

Your Affiliate Network can be one of the most profitable areas to spend your time. In a small online business, it is a great thing to pay tens of thousands of dollars in commissions each year to Affiliates in exchange for Affiliates sending paying customers from links on their websites. The beauty of an Affiliate network is that you only pay commissions to your network when payment or performance is received.

These traffic driving networks typically have a small cost to join, but offer you access to a large group of members who specialize in promoting Affiliate offers to their web visitors. The members can make an excellent living off the commissions and bounties paid by customers of the affiliate network. Run a search on "affiliate networks" to find a current listing.

6. Repeat Visits

A fundamental part of your planning is around how to attract Visitors back to your website for repeat visits. This will dramatically increase your traffic counts and is very cost efficient. How do you encourage people to visit your site again without a huge investment?

- ✓ Bookmarking – make it easy for people to bookmark your website for future visits. Web browsers have built-in features to make this easy for visitors, so suggest that people bookmark your website in your copy.

- ✓ Daily Winners – create a Game of Chance that has a daily prize structure that requires entering daily to win.

- ✓ Content – offer fresh content on your website periodically to attract repeat visits. Some websites offer a featured article or quote of the day to encourage repeat visits.

- ✓ Email Reminders – for those people who sign-up to receive emails from you, create reasons and incentives to click through links in your email messages to visit your website.

✓ Daily or Weekly Specials – offer fresh deals and discounts on a periodic basis. Steeper discounts on your featured deals translate into higher repeat visit rates.

7. Directory Registration

The Internet has a number of directory services that help people find information that is of interest to them. Registering URLs on these directories provides a decent source of ongoing traffic.

Website Directories – A popular directory is the Open Directory (DMOZ.org), a free directory edited by volunteer editors. Other popular directories include Yahoo.com and Google Local.

Sweepstakes Directories – when you run a sweepstakes, there is a community of millions of avid sweepstakes players, or "sweepers" as they are called in the industry. Register your sweepstakes on these directories, as these consumers regularly buy goods and services such as travel, cat food and cars. Run a Google search on "sweepstakes directories" to visit.

Shopping Directories – these directories contain links to products offered for sale. Often, a retailer will upload their catalog to the directory for comparison shopping purposes. Some of these directories are free, some charge retailers for loading their products and other directories earn a commission off of each sale referred from the directory (similar to an Affiliate marketing partner).

THE BRANDING PARADOX:

Brand Building and How It Relates to Conversion Marketing

(Below the Line)

So, what is the Conversion Marketer's "Branding Paradox?" A friend of mine who works at Microsoft's MSN division recently told me that the Branding Paradox sounds more like the title of a movie than a chapter in a marketing book. Despite her "constructive feedback," here is what I've learned from running call-to-action or below-the-line marketing campaigns: There is an inverse relationship between the goal of achieving "top of mind" brand recognition (above-the-line) and success in achieving eCommerce Conversions.

The reason is that in traditional marketing terms, the activities related to Branding sometimes conflict with activities generating sales revenue. Branding campaigns are typically executed in television, radio and print with measuring sticks such as top-of-mind recall and unaided brand awareness. These ads can sometimes be designed to create an emotional connection with a Brand. Direct Response advertisers measure of success are directly tied to sales goals like cost per lead, cost per conversion or revenue per visitor.

First let's understand the traditional definitions of Promotions and Branding. Here is a quick review of each definition.

1. Promotion: A promotion is a short-term incentive marketing campaign designed to stimulate or modify a consumer's buying behavior. By definition, a promotion creates fear of loss, one of the most powerful motivators in the marketplace. It moves people to buy now because the opportunity may not last.

2. Branding: A brand is the symbolic embodiment of all the information a company uses around which to create associations and expectations. Obviously this is a bit more subtle and complex than a Promotion. We could fill entire volumes with philosophies of Branding. Simply put, Branding includes the essence of what you're offering – the messaging, logo, color schemes, symbols, fonts, sounds or any other image-related concepts associated with the soul of your company. It's about mojo, the personality of what your company brings to the table. Branding is what sets apart how consumers feel about your company, products or services.

In eCommerce-oriented companies however, the line between Branding, Promotion and Direct Response Marketing has blurred. Often, eCommerce marketers must accomplish branding repetition and call-to-action promotional marketing activities simultaneously. eCommerce departments, especially at smaller companies, are proving that you can manage marketing campaigns which accomplish often competing goals.

Background on Marketing Departments:

Large companies with well-established brand names hire thousands of employees in various Marketing disciplines. These various departments range from Direct Marketing, Product Marketing, and Channel Marketing to Public Relations, Retention Marketing, Promotional Marketing and Branding. In these large marketing departments, there is a chasm between the teams who steward a company's Brand and those who practice the Conversion Marketing arts. The Brand-building activity is considered separate and distinct from most other forms of marketing activity.

The way the consumer sees a Brand marketer's impact is typically in national media campaigns designed to promote a feeling associated with a Brand. Notice your own response to which Brands comes to mind when you see phrases like:

"Oh what a Feeling" (Toyota)

"Just Do It" (Nike)

"King of Beers" (Budweiser)

"Because I'm worth it" [L'Oreal}

"The Next 100 Years" [Neimann-Marcus}

The Brand Manager has the responsibility to generate Creative Repetition in order to plant their message firmly into the subconscious of the target audience. When advertising a brand image, typically one does not promote price in these campaigns or use other call-to-action messages such as coupons, offers or limited-time price discounts.

The Brand message is purely focused on creating a favorable image in the mind of the consumer and repeating that image in order to create a permanence in the minds of the target consumer. Brand managers also are responsible for brand consistency, making sure brand quality requirements are upheld across thousands of venues.

This backgrounder is to help illustrate the point that the large company Brand marketer will have little to do with Conversion Marketing. The Brand marketer's mentality is often oriented to the long-term impact on the image of the Brand, while other Marketing Departments have direct revenue responsibility.

A rule of thumb for allocating a Marketing budget corporately is to spend 15% of dollars allocated to Marketing above the line on brand advertising and 85% below the line on sales-related marketing activities. These percentages vary widely depending on the type of product sold, the sales cycle, maturity of a brand, how many well-established sales channels exist, along with a host of other factors.

This background on the structure of Marketing departments is important to understand the phenomenon that the Conversion Marketer calls the Branding Paradox. In order for the Conversion Marketer to have maximum impact, they too need to think carefully about the Brand image that is being communicated to people who give permission to receive ongoing communications within the Conversions Loop. For those Marketers operating eCommerce websites in small-to-mid-size companies, the task of Branding will fall squarely on the shoulders of the Conversion Marketer.

Branding must be taken seriously and may seem counterintuitive when structuring your Conversion Marketing campaigns. The Conversion Marketer's primary job is to drive sales revenue. However, before the consumer will make a purchase decision, a bond of trust needs to be established.

As a rule, fewer than two percent of consumers (and often less than one percent) will make a purchase decision upon the first exposure to a website that they have not heard of or not yet conducted a buying transaction. This bond of trust is achieved through Creative Repetition of a clear, simple message.

> *It takes three to seven exposures to your message before subconscious awareness is achieved in the minds of your target audience.*

As previously mentioned, it takes seven exposures to your message before subconscious awareness is achieved in the minds of your target audience. Therefore the Conversion Marketer needs to craft a Branding strategy in their communications campaigns in order to achieve ultimate success.

Let's see where the Branding component of your Conversion Marketing strategy belongs in the process. An important question for the Conversion Marketer is establishing when the brand-building activities end in the Conversions Loop, and when it is appropriate to start asking for the sale.

The answer depends on your company, your products and services. Typically Conversion Marketing activities should start after you have exposed your messages to each individual a minimum of three times. Might customers be ready to buy earlier than the third exposure? Based on the dynamics of your industry and the familiarity of your Brand, only you will know. Some guidelines for the frequency of email communications, along with a comprehensive look at planning email campaigns, are included later for reference.

A mega Brand product, such as a soft drink or designer jeans, will have clear lines of distinction where Brand building ends and Conversion Marketing begins. These companies promote the promise of their Brands through mass media advertising channels. They then rely on multiple channels of distribution to create sales conversions such as in the case of a soft drink manufacturer where conversions are achieved via distributors, bottlers, stadium concessions, supermarkets, drug stores, convenience stores and so on.

A challenge faced by many megabrands is the rapidly changing media viewing patterns by different segments of the population. Twenty years ago, the big Brand marketers could reach large percentages of their target audience through mass media channels with a handful of network television, outdoor and radio advertising vendors.

Today the opportunity to reach that same percentage of an audience is infinitely more complex. For example, let's look at reaching the demographic of young males, 18-25 years old. This group is highly sought after for long-term branding as their future Brand loyalty is valuable over the long-term to marketers. Today's challenge with Branding to the demographic of young males is finding them through mass media channels as user-generated media and gaming systems have rapidly drawn the attention of this demographic away from television.

Where young men spend their discretionary time is also changing rapidly. When a target audience gravitates to new forms of media quickly, this creates challenges when planning long-term media campaign strategies. Rapidly changing creative technology to reach your audience is a fundamental element for today's media buyer. Each new venue of advertising requires separate and unique creative materials along with technology vendors capable of serving ads in these environments.

Here are a handful of methods a marketer might deploy to reach the demographic of the young male at the time of this printing. Imagine you're in charge of creating specific advertisements, or spots, for each type of media listed below:

- ✓ Video sharing sites, like YouTube
- ✓ Social Networks like Facebook
- ✓ In-game advertising for Xbox, Sony and Nintendo games
- ✓ Cable TV channels (hundreds of channels)

✓ Network TV

✓ Radio

✓ Print – magazines

✓ Outdoor – billboards, bus signs, subway signs

What makes an excellent Outdoor campaign will rarely translate to what works in the venue where young males are increasingly spending their time; viewing funny, shocking or entertaining videos.

Here is an example of the structure of a perfectly executed Conversion Marketing campaign run by NISSAN to support the launch of a car targeting young males. The campaign targets a highly desirable market of young males who spend thousands of dollars "tuning their ride," or customizing their car for looks, the sound of their exhaust system, increasing horsepower or installing a pounding stereo system.

The "Conversions" for Nissan, in this example, are managed by a large network of independent auto dealerships, which have little exposure to the corporate marketing department of Nissan. This campaign illustrates how a large company with an indirect influence on their sales team can leverage mass media with a carefully-crafted Conversion Marketing campaign to create sales conversions.

The Nissan campaign was built around a Sony PlayStation video game featuring the hot new car. Players can tune the car and race their friends in the gaming environment, all with thumping, high-energy music in the background. The goals of the campaign were twofold: 1) to build awareness of the car, and 2) to create "Interested Visitors" by attracting them into the showroom for a test drive, where the dealers are trained to produce Conversions.

The Nissan campaign started with an email broadcast to an in-house list, along with a mass-media campaign including TV, outdoor billboards, print advertising, online advertising, and email list rental. A weekly reminder email was sent to all registered participants with reminders to participate in the online components of an Instant Win game of chance with hundreds of prizes awarded on-the-spot to contestants.

Each participant in the campaign also was entered into a sweepstakes drawing with the Grand Prize of the new car.

By the way, if you are ever in the position of planning a big Game of Chance, using a car that inspires your audience is an excellent strategy, as cars get very high response rates in sweepstakes campaigns. Each participant in the Nissan campaign was also given a chance to instantly win a Sony PlayStation. Finally, each participant was encouraged to tell-a-friend (viral marketing) with gifts of T-shirts when five friends entered the contest.

Finally, all the leads captured in this campaign were emailed to the nearest automotive dealership (sorted by Zip/Postal Code) for follow up by local salespeople. At the conclusion of the campaign, each participant who opted-in for email communications was sent a special invitation to visit their local Nissan dealer to pick up a free T-Shirt and take a test drive of the car, thereby closing the Conversions Loop methodology for the campaign.

This campaign was perfectly designed to create awareness of the new vehicle, build an email database for Creative Repetition and to create sales conversions via a promotional campaign designed to inspire young males to fully engage with the Nissan Brand.

Typically the larger the Brand name, the more complexity exists in the sales channels where Conversions are achieved. Large companies may not have the ability to tightly control their Conversion Marketing campaign due to the distance, in terms of sales channels, between the corporate sales team and the end user of the product.

For instance, look at a pharmaceutical company. They rely on referrals from physicians to prescribe new medications or medical procedures to their patients, maybe several thousand patients per year per physician. The process of convincing extremely busy physicians to learn new techniques and drug treatments requires an army of field representatives to visit physicians and hospitals to provide awareness and training. However, the end users of the products are consumers. This dynamic creates an indirect relationship between the sales team and the end user.

Smaller companies may have relatively unknown Brand names but a big advantage that they own a direct-sale relationship with end users of their products and services. The closer your company can move its transactional capabilities to the end-user, the greater the advantages in your ability to win brand trust.

Having your Branding strategy and your Conversion Marketing strategy integrated into one campaign, via the Conversions Loop methodology, will dramatically increase your marketing effectiveness.

Costs of achieving brand loyalty

Intuitively, it makes sense that it is more cost-effective to win the minds of hundreds of thousands or even millions of end users through mass-media campaigns. The cost per Brand impression is the lowest in mass media applications, such as running national television spots during sporting events. However, a high-cost barrier to entry exists in launching national-branding campaigns. Generating creative TV spots can run millions of dollars per spot.

Using the Conversion Loop methodology online, Brand loyalty can be achieved cost-effectively by automating technology to win brand trust. Highly effective Conversion Marketers will have segmented Conversion campaigns for different types of products and services, so the Brand messaging is as relevant as possible to the end user's needs.

Branding research supports the notion that multiple brand repetitions is a key element to achieving brand trust. The Conversions Loop methodology for Conversion Marketers combines the principles of brand building along with tight integration of your sales conversion goals, all wrapped-up into one campaign.

After a Visitor to your website has opted-in to your Conversions Loop campaign, they become an Interested Visitor. These Interested Visitors are exposed to your company, Brand or service a minimum of three times and are now ready to cross the threshold of converting to a Customer.

THE PSYCHOLOGY OF CONVERSION

What makes Consumers buy Online

The average consumer is exposed to 3,000 advertising messages - A DAY. With this much information overload, how can you succeed in getting your message across to your audience?

In 1995, the amount of content (books, articles, radio, TV, blogs, etc.) produced in a 24-hour period would take the average person a LIFETIME to review. Today, enough content is produced EACH SECOND for a lifetime of consumption by the average human being.

With the amount of content choices so overwhelming, it is important to understand the psychology of information processing in order to build a Conversion Marketing strategy that works effectively.

So, let's start looking at how the human brain processes information and deals with an overload of stimuli. The mind will create filters when processing information. These filters act as barriers to all the messages competing for mindshare. These barriers are the things that keep us sane. Understanding how to work WITH these psychological barriers is key to selling success.

We all put up barriers to messaging, called Communication Barriers. We look for messages that confirm our outlook, our worldview, our philosophy on life, our interests, etc. We filter out messages that we deem irrelevant to our viewpoints. Let's explore how to view the Conversions Loop in terms of breaking through these Communication Barriers, such as crafting messages that are consistent with the worldview of your target audience.

Importance of Identifying your Target Audience

Understanding exactly WHO your target audience is will be the next step in the Psychology of Conversion. Once you have your target audience in mind, you can then cater your campaign to an individual (or set of individuals in your mind's eye). We start by establishing the Demographic profile of an audience by formulating a clear picture of who our audience is:

- ✓ Age

- ✓ Education profile

- ✓ Gender

- ✓ Geographic location

- ✓ Marital status

- ✓ Household income

- ✓ Residence (renter, home owner, condo dweller, etc.)

Every now and then, I have made classic marketing mistakes. Let me tell you about a recent miscalculation in order to help you prevent making similar missteps related to demographic profiling.

A while back, I created an eCommerce website using a dark graphic treatment. After operating this site for a year, we discovered that the typical consumer of this service was 75% female. According to design specialists who deal in color theory, using dark graphics are a detriment to attracting and motivating this demographic.

By changing the user interface to softer colors and more descriptive copywriting, we were able to generate a 50% increase in our Visitor to Buyer ratios. The questions I ask myself include: How much revenue did I sacrifice as a result of this design misstep? How many advertising dollars did I waste driving the wrong target audience to this website?

Next, once you can visualize your target audience(s), it is essential to understand their outlook on life, their view of themselves, their recreational pursuits and other factors that make them tick. Marketers call this the Psychographic Profile of your target audience.

To understand what a Psychographic profile looks like, here are questions to ask to help understand your customer's personality, values, attitudes, interests, or lifestyles:

- ✓ What do they do in their spare time? For example, there are powerful correlations between software professionals and road bikes, between mathematicians and music, between mechanics and viewing motor sports and between corporate executives and golf.

- ✓ What are their beliefs?

- ✓ What is their social status?

- ✓ What lifestyle do they lead?

- ✓ What strong opinions do they hold?

- ✓ What are their values?

Once you have completed your demographic and psychographic profiles on the ideal target audience(s), the next principle to add to the knowledge base on Conversion Marketing is the concept of SOCIAL INFLUENCE.

Social Influence is a deep-seated human desire to appear consistent with what we have already done in the past, as well as commitments that define the things we represent in the future. This human desire is so deep-rooted, that we will even do things that are contrary to our financial best interests in order to act consistently with what we feel we represent.

The principle of Social Influence means we will convince ourselves of the correctness of a decision, even if the decision is not in-line with our best interests. So, to stay true to our nature to be consistent with our inner convictions, the human mind goes into an "mental auto-pilot mode" in order to speed up our internal decision-making process, all in the blink of an eye. This fundamental aspect of human nature helps us process the bombardment of messages by disregarding messages inconsistent with our inner convictions, worldview/philosophy.

How can you structure your Conversion Marketing messaging to conform to the "mental auto-pilot" mode of your target audience?

> **FIRST:** clearly understand your target audience – both their demographic and psychographic profile.

> **SECOND:** create messaging and imagery that is consistent with the outlook of your target audience. For instance, if you are targeting Empty Nesters (50-63 year olds) you would use inspirational messages and images consistent with their outlook: happy grandchildren, RV travel to National Parks, beach vacations, spas or wine tasting.

> **THIRD:** pick your "call to action" eCommerce strategy from a list of options that support the desire to be consistent with your target audiences' nature. Pick the appropriate online Conversion tool listed in the previous chapter. Then, carefully review the Conversion Tips listed in this chapter for techniques that influence buying behavior.

Psychological Conversion Tips

This series of Conversion Tips originates from carefully researched psychological studies on human behavior, which have proven to generate hundreds of millions of dollars in eCommerce conversions by skilled Conversion Marketers. Think carefully about each Tip and how it can be adapted into your eCommerce environment. Don't be surprised to see a spike in conversion rates when you implement these powerful psychological triggers in the design of your campaigns.

CONVERSION TIP #1 – START SMALL

If your ultimate goal is to sell something large and relatively expensive, it is rare that your company will achieve success in an eCommerce environment on the first, second or even third visit to your website. Therefore, you need to build a bond of trust with your audience by performing a small transaction, and then build your way into a large commitment. For instance, if you are selling a $25,000 Mediterranean cruise package, think about offering a short weekend trip as a trial to build trust and whet the appetite of your audience.

CONVERSION TIP #2 - STEPPED COMMITMENTS

Create a gradual series of commitments, tapping into the latent "power of consistency" behavior in the human mind. Set the stage for creating a series of automatic conversion behavior on your website. Start with small commitments such as opting-in for a newsletter, direct-mail campaign or other informational series of messages. These small commitments will impact the self-image of your audience, and will help them see their viewpoint as consistent with that of your company.

CONVERSION TIP #3 - THE MAGIC OF WRITTEN DECLARATIONS

Recently, I developed a website in the industry of Audio Publishing. One consistent message coming from this industry's leading celebrity speakers like Brian Tracy, Chris Widener and Zig Ziglar, is in setting clear and definable goals. There is great power in written goals, proven in study after study. One study found that two percent of Harvard graduates have written goals. These two percent of graduates consistently out earn their non-goal-setting counterparts by significant margins. Why? It gets back to the human need to be consistent with one's beliefs. The act of writing a goal deeply seats this commitment in the mind. So, how do you get people to make written declarations online? Here are a few ideas:

- ✓ Testimonial Sweepstakes: offer your target audience a chance to win a big prize by submitting a testimonial to your product/service, such as a "Why I like _____" statement.

This helps your audience go on record endorsing your product or service.

✓ Easter Egg Campaign – an "Easter egg" is a hidden message within a website or product. Run a contest where you prompt people to find your "Easter egg" message (i.e. as hidden on the back of the product label, nested in an email newsletter, nested within your home page, or in icons placed throughout your website). Have the contest be contingent on finding the message and submitting it online. Craft your message so that it states a positive testimonial for your product. When submitted, it enters them in the contest and also embeds the positive message in the contestant's mind.

Examples: Craft your hidden messages as a written declaration supporting your product.

✓ I love this product!

✓ Your product rocks!

Psychological studies have shown that people who make written declarations will more assertively defend these positions than research subjects who only made mental commitments. These strong convictions hold for the subjects who made written declarations even when they were shown evidence to challenge their position.

CONVERSION TIP #4 – SOCIAL PROOF

Publish testimonials from people who fit the demographic or psychographic profile of your target audience. The idea is to show support for your products/services by people who look "just like me." Use integrity with this tip, and ask your best customers for real testimonials. You will be surprised what people have to say, and you just may learn a thing or two about your product/service.

The more you can demonstrate that many people support your idea/product/service as correct, the more others will perceive your idea/product/service as correct. Think of the highest profile success story of this technique the next time you see a McDonald's sign showing how many billions of customers have been served.

CONVERSION TIP #5 – EXTRA EFFORT TO JOIN A CLUB

The more effort that a person applies into a commitment, the greater is your ability to influence the attitude and beliefs of club members.

How can you apply this principle to an eCommerce environment?

Offer a free newsletter, but require the extra effort of a double opt-in to join the newsletter (see Chapter 10 on the definition of double opt-in).

When launching a new website, communicate a compelling promise or purpose that membership will achieve but require a waiting period for "approval" before validating the membership. This impression of exclusivity increases the perceived value of your site. Think of the example of a waiting period before joining a country club, or a review from a membership committee before new applications are accepted.

Require a referral from an already existing member before you allow new members to "join the club." This was successful for Google's launch of its Gmail service to compete with Microsoft's Hotmail version of a free email account. Not only was a Gmail account sought-after, it was a badge of prestige for early users because they were on the inside elite of the high-tech community.

CONVERSION TIP #6 – LOSS LEADER

Offering a loss leader is a tried-and-true method of attracting new business in the hyper-competitive, brick & mortar retail world. Grocery stores operate loss leaders all the time – for example in North America discounted turkeys around Thanksgiving, discounted soft drinks prior to July 4th and candy discounts prior to Halloween.

What are the biggest shopping holidays in your country or region? These deeply discounted items attract shoppers for the Loss Leader, which is made up in the volume of other items purchased during the same season. Think about your product profile and offering seasonal discounts on highly popular items as a way of attracting new customers.

CONVERSION TIP #7 – ASK AN EXPERT

The influence of a well-known expert in your field can project a positive influence on your company. Offer a Blog, where your website visitors can interact with an Expert/Celebrity/Leader in your field. The value of the interaction and ability to read unscripted feedback, plus the residual benefit of repeat traffic to your website, can have a very positive impact on your visitors.

CONVERSION TIP #8 – REFERRALS

Research has proven that people prefer to say "Yes" to a purchase when coming from someone we know and/or like.

Provide an incentive item for people who refer a required number of friends to your website to join your newsletter or purchase items. Here are a few working examples from past campaigns offered by various Internet marketers.

1. Get 10 additional sweepstakes entries for each friend you refer who enters a sweepstakes for a free trip to New Orleans. This was deployed by the State tourism commission in Louisiana for years to build a database of hundreds of thousands of people interested in travel to Louisiana.

2. Earn a free movie rental certificate for every five new newsletter opt-ins. One marketer was able to save 50% on new customer acquisition costs by leveraging this technique.

3. Get a free sample package of Proctor & Gamble personal care products for each friend referred to a sweepstakes. This referral structure served double duty to accomplish the objective of gaining new traffic, newsletter opt-ins and achieve the objectives of product trial.

CONVERSION TIP #9 – ATTRACTIVENESS FACTOR

People naturally tend to respond positively to people and graphic design elements that match their tastes. If you use a celebrity spokesperson to promote your items, then select one that inspires your target audience.

If you market items where it is cost prohibitive to leverage a celebrity spokesperson, then spend some of your energy on the graphic design of your website that closely aligns with the "attractiveness factor" of your target audience. Think carefully about the color scheme you choose, the design elements and style of copywriting used to stimulate the senses of your target audience.

Celebrity Endorsements: One example of a major search engine using the "Attractiveness Factor" to stimulate their target audience was a major search engine that was focused on attracting young males from 18-29 years old. They ran a sweepstakes where each entry earned a chance to meet a very attractive 19-year-old tennis sensation.

The winner of this sweepstakes was a 21-year-old college student, who brought four friends to meet the tennis star while on the beach during a swimsuit modeling photo session. We were all greatly amused when the winner of the sweepstakes presented the tennis star with a bouquet of roses to win her eye! If you are curious how the tennis star responded, she politely declined the offer with a wink and a smile.

Models: To create a positive association with your products, it can be effective and economical for smaller companies to pose an attractive model next to product images in your online catalog.

CONVERSION TIP #10 – SOCIAL RESPONSIBILITY: LEVERAGING THE "US-VERSUS-THEM" PHENOMENOM

People have the tendency to mentally group themselves into associations with clubs, charities, movements and organizations. The obvious illustration of this phenomenon is rooting for the home team in football or baseball. Residents of cities where teams reside adopt an Us-Versus-Them mentality on game day and will feverishly cheer for their home team.

This phenomenon can be activated by giving to charitable organizations that share an affinity with your target audience. The association your company has can align you with common goals of your target audience. Some people choose to buy certain products because of their associations with organizations in which they strongly believe in.

One company that promotes language learning software offers five percent of the proceeds from each purchase to support "green" initiatives for environmental causes. This company has proven this tool to be effective selling "National Geographic" software products, where satisfied consumers have indicated their purchase decision based solely on the company's social stance to charitable giving! So pick a charity that you feel good about that also aligns with your target audience and start giving back.

A local karate studio organizes a quarterly "Pizza and Game Night" at the studio where parents drop off kids and enjoy a night out on the town. One hundred percent of the money collected goes to building elaborate playsets for orphaned children in disadvantaged areas. One reason they succeed is by helping their customers participate in socially responsible activities. With programs which appeal to a cause bigger than oneself, it is no coincidence that this karate studio is one of the top five largest single-location karate studios in North America.

CONVERSION TIP #11 – THE DRAW OF "AUTHORITY"

Authority figures can have a strong influence on your target audience. Interesting studies have been run where people have been encouraged to perform activities contrary to their beliefs and values based solely on the influence of an "authority figure" telling them that the actions are justified.

Notice the types of Hollywood celebrities that are hired to endorse products. Just recently, I saw an actor who plays a respectable President of the United States in a popular television series. In this television spot the actor is promoting "You are in good hands..." for a large insurance company. Actors who play physicians are often used to promote products/services of large advertisers as the positive impression people have towards physicians, in general, will extend to the advertiser's message.

In an eCommerce environment, leveraging authority figures can have a measurable effect on your conversion rates with website visitors. People will inherently trust the message coming from these celebrity figures.

In the absence of the big-budget dollars to hire a celebrity, send an email to a leading authority in your industry that presented at a recent trade event or authored a book relevant to your industry. Many experts, including professional speakers and authors, are MORE than happy to associate their message to your audience, as the goal of public relations is always top of mind for speakers and authors.

CONVERSION TIP #12 – GRAPHIC DESIGN

In the physical world people respond to non-verbal cues, such as the title before someone's name, clothes, uniforms or visible status symbols (cars, homes, watches, jewelry, designer logos), that communicate authority. In the eCommerce environment, you can communicate the trust associated with such visible cues via the graphic design of your website. Carefully pick color schemes and design elements that support your product.

CONVERSION TIP #13 – SCARCITY CREATES DEMAND

While studying for my undergraduate degree in Economics, the principle of "Scarcity creates Demand" was taught as yet another dry lesson from the thick Economics textbook. When it is perceived that a product is in high demand and there is limited supply, people tend to stock-up or purchase in advance of their need.

Here are a few tips for creating Demand by communicating a scarce availability of product and/or price (which Economists called "Artificial Scarcity"):

✓ Limited time discount – act now while the discount applies

✓ Limited quantity – buy a limited supply of discounted products, i.e. available to the first 50 customers

✓ Commemoratives – Artists, by creating numbered series of collectable works, are the masters of this conversion technique. Authors also leverage this phenomenon by offering a limited quantity of signed books or by organizing "signing events" at local bookstores and trade events.

CONVERSION TIP #14 – SCARCITY PLUS RIVALRY

The concept of creating scarcity with the added element of a rivalry for the scarce goods is the essence of the eBay auction-based business model. A limited quantity of items plus a huge network of deal-hunters are the perfect convergence of the Scarcity + Rivalry principle to stimulate demand for conversions.

eBay auctions offer valued items in limited discounts for a limited time, typically offered at a VERY low initial asking price. As rivals for these discounted products start to compete, a frenzy of activity is initiated that would not normally exist for the same item at full price or even at a reasonable discount. As rivals become emotionally involved in the purchase process, they will bid up the price of items often to the full price (or beyond) in their quest to "win" the auction. The Emotional Involvement associated with the rivalry can have a powerful impact on your conversion rates.

> *The Emotional Involvement associated with the rivalry can have a powerful impact on your conversion rates.*

While I was in college, I posted a classified ad for a popular-sized carpet used in the building where I lived. As it happens, two motivated buyers showed up to buy the carpet at the exact same time, giving me a front-row seat on consumer behavior related to Scarcity + Rivalry. I watched these two potential buyers bid up the carpet fifty percent over the asking price in order to take advantage of this scarce item. How can this principle apply to your business?

✓ Think about creating a store on eBay or Craigslist to promote a limited supply of your goods and services at a discount. The stores are relatively intuitive to set up and populate your catalog. You will gain the substantial advantage of gaining access to the massive amount of traffic going to these ecommerce websites daily. If the process of setting up your own stores on these websites is too time-consuming or daunting, there are a number of people who are experienced eBay practitioners who offer the service of selling your products through these online retailers for a percentage of revenue, a percentage of gross margin, or by buying your goods at wholesale discounts. eBay also has a network of Trading Assistants who will train you on the subtle tips and tricks of selling on eBay. These Trading Assistants can be found in many major cities for a fairly reasonable hourly fee.

CONVERSION TIP #15 – PRODUCT COLLECTIONS

If you offer a catalog of products with a wide array of choices, you can simplify the decision-making process for your customers by offering pre-packaged products, often sold at a discount. It is proven that a certain percentage of the population will buy a larger dollar amount of product if it will save them time and money sorting through all the options of products on your website.

One successful online retailer will do 10% of their business overall offering a $999 package deal on all their products (which individually sell for $10-$25 separately). A discount offered on the package deal can be structured to leverage this technique properly.

CONVERSION TIP #16 – COGNITIVE DISSONANCE

"Cognitive Dissonance" is a marketing term which describes conflicting thoughts that some consumers experience after making a big purchase. When confronted with a big purchase decision, some consumers will feel a sense of regret called "post-purchase dissonance" for making the purchase, spending the money or discovering information that makes them uncomfortable with their purchase.

Techniques can be used to help minimize this effect, and help increase conversion rates on your website prior to purchase. Here are tips on how to structure an eCommerce site to minimize this "objection":

- ✓ Create a "No-hassle" return policy

- ✓ Offer a 100% money back guarantee

- ✓ Provide easy access to Customer Service, via email or a toll-free number

- ✓ Offering a credit card payment option helps alleviate this concern as consumers know they can dispute charges and receive a credit on their account from their credit card issuers.

In our increasingly fast-paced, information-laden society, your target audience's ability to make a buying decision for your product/service requires creating prompts that trigger a normal and predictable feeling within the mind of your audience.

The more reliable the cues you can provide in your eCommerce environment will help break-down the natural barriers we use to protect our minds from the bombardment of information presented each day.

As I write this chapter, I'm sipping an espresso in a coffee shop in a small resort town deep in the heart of the Washington State wine country. In being intentional about letting a few marketing messages penetrate my conscious mind, I can count at least 10 marketing messages competing for my attention at a casual glance (Coca-Cola, Good Humor ice cream, flip flops, sun glasses, resort wear, etc.). Your job is to create a mentally comfortable experience to your website visitors in order to capture attention, gain permission and start the Creative Repetition of your Branding message.

ACQUISITION STRATEGIES

When I started in the Interactive Advertising business, the business of acquiring new customers could be quite expensive. Buying high volume ad buys from major publishers like Yahoo! and MSN required a minimum budget in the tens of thousands/month.

We live in a great time. Historically, the conversion tracking software tools to track acquisitions described in this chapter would cost a business $500,000 to license and would require a dedicated team of software developers to operate the system. In fact, just setting up the server hardware to run this technology cost more than $250,000 when eCommerce was in its infancy.

I met a sharp guy named Monte who helped architect our server farm, using his extensive expertise on database technology gleaned from years working for IBM. Monte and I became close friends, and when we look back at the infrastructure that we built to support an online technology company, we shake our heads at the amount of time, manpower and resources it took to support this business. The last time I saw Monte was at a ballet fundraiser, right before he was heading to Transylvania (yes, for real!) to set up a call center for Microsoft.

Today, a complete suite of powerful acquisition tracking technology is available to even the smallest advertisers, for about $20 per month! These systems have more power to track conversions than the $500,000 software....for the same price as a business lunch today. I'll outline where to get these tools and how to use them by the end of this chapter.

In one of my start-up companies, one of our goals was to win business with large customers despite the small size of the start-up. With my Interactive Advertising start-up company, our lucky break came when we landed a large media buying agency called aQuantive, which was purchased by Microsoft for an eye-popping $6 billion.

To get our four-person company in front of this customer, we visited their office tower one cold morning with an espresso cart, a barista and a box of custom-imprinted coffee mugs. The mugs were printed with both our company logo and the customer's logo. Of course, the mugs and barista on a cold Seattle morning were a brilliant combination.

The sales pitch was a "dog-and-pony" show to tell the employees about our services, while handing out steaming-hot lattes in the customized mugs. The mugs were designed to associate our young brand with the established brand of the potential client. Next, we met with the executive team to demonstrate our expertise in setting up and measuring the conversions from online sweepstakes campaigns. As a result, we won a contract to create a sweepstakes for one of their mid-size customers who manufactured customized golf clubs.

The campaign was a success and the business flourished from that point forward. What was enjoyable about working with this customer was the sophistication of their advertising tracking software. Online advertising executives like to measure everything. We won the business as our systems helped enhance the measurement of the cost per acquisition for their clients. At that time, aQuantive's advertising customers were required to spend $25,000/month to become a client, who then enjoyed their robust campaign reporting to support big advertising campaigns. Some of their clients had multi-million monthly ad budgets.

aQuantive's stock options for employees became quite valuable. The last I heard from our client was that she was sailing around the world in her sailboat. Developing your Conversion Marketing skills can be a valuable asset to your business as well.

The Art of Acquisition

In this chapter, we explore a variety of acquisition strategies and will help you determine which tools are appropriate for your industry. We will also answer common questions about how to configure the campaigns for maximum effectiveness.

When planning the best type of customer acquisition tool to use for your business, use this quick-reference guide. This guide is organized by industry, which can be a lifesaver if you are servicing clients as an Agency. Keep this resource near your desk, as this section can save you incredible amounts of time and will help stretch your marketing budget.

Picking the right tool for each campaign is critically important. For instance, a luxury brand like Mercedes Benz would rarely offer a coupon. Or, it is unlikely that an industrial equipment manufacturer with 50 customers would advertise an Instant Win offer.

Evaluate the three industry segments below and determine the appropriate ranking for your industry segment based on the principles outlined in this chapter. The numbers in the cart below provide an index of how appropriate each of these tactics can be for your industry. On a scale of 1-10, a ranking of 10 means that this acquisition tactic may be highly relevant for your industry.

Effectiveness Index, by Industry Type

TYPE of Acquisition Tactics	Consumer Goods (transactional)	Business to Business	Luxury Goods (expensive)	Your Industry (fill-in) ???
Coupon with Registration	8	7	2	
Sweepstakes	6	4	3	
Refer-A-Friend incentive	10	6	9	
Free Gift with Action	8	8	8	
Self Liquidator	6	3	5	
Instant Win Game	7	4	3	
Scavenger Hunt	8	6	6	
Free Content	6	8	7	
Industry Research	2	8	4	
Free Trial	8	9	3	

*The Effectiveness Index by industry type is measured on a scale of 1 (low effectiveness) to 10 (high effectiveness)

Remember as discussed in the AIDA chart, it takes time and engagement to create DESIRE in the mind of consumers. Running promotional campaigns to draw traffic and engagement with your Brand is important before your Target Audience is receptive to conversion messages.

Games of Chance

Sweepstakes and Instant Win games are the primary types of Games of Chance. These games are unique, in that there is "no consideration" (or no cost) to enter the competition. Games of Chance are legal in all 50 states, although registration of your game is required in NY and FL if the overall prize structure of your game exceeds $5,000.

There are many reasons to offer a Game of Chance. These reasons include:

- ✓ Increased sales conversions

- ✓ Data capture (or permission marketing)

- ✓ Attracting new visitors

- ✓ Creating excitement for upcoming events

- ✓ Driving traffic to your website.

Capturing data in a Game of Chance is an art form. Be sensitive to trying to capture too much data in exchange for a sweepstakes entry. Always ask yourself how you plan to use the data you capture and if each question you ask is worth the drop-off rates associated with each additional question you ask. Remember that your Target Audience has a subconscious instinct for comparing the amount of time it takes to answer your survey questions relative to their desire to win your Grand Prize.

As a quick reference, here is the structure of a typical online sweepstakes to help save time in setting-up a campaign.

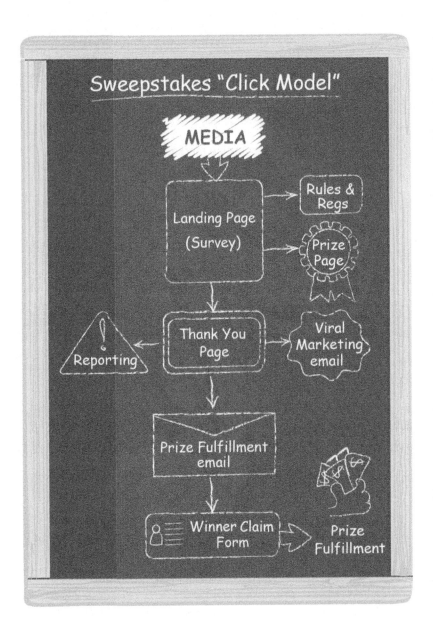

Once your Game of Chance is set-up, keeping track of your results is key to achieving your online marketing goals outlined in Chapter Three. Here is a practical at-a-glance reference tool for keeping track of your successes.

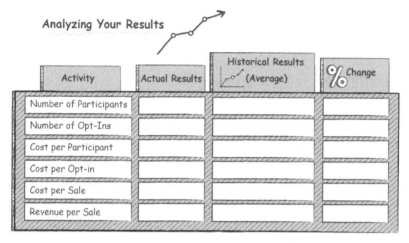

Activity	Actual Results	Historical Results (Average)	% Change
Number of Participants			
Number of Opt-Ins			
Cost per Participant			
Cost per Opt-in			
Cost per Sale			
Revenue per Sale			

Download an Excel version of this Conversion Calculator at http://www.conversionmarketingbook.com/resources.html

Create an ongoing log of each campaign to help set future goals and track progress.

If your tracking system enables tracking for specific promotional URLs, what the industry calls Split Testing, you can track the Revenue per Sale for each campaign while making minor adjustments to the campaign creative. Your creative variables include images, colors copy, offer, price, etc. Google AdWords has excellent Conversion Tracking technology, using invisible tracking pixels placed into your shopping cart software. This is available free to active Google advertisers and Google Analytics users. A tracking pixel will look for "cookies" placed on a Visitor's device when they visit your website after clicking on ads sold by Google (or other third parties in their network). For a summary of how to implement Conversion Tracking pixels, search Google for "tracking pixels" to describe how this works.

Interestingly, the same advertising tracking software described is available from Google AdWords to advertisers spending less than $1 a day (compared to what used to cost $750,000 to set-up). Thereby, an interior decorator, dance studio or personal trainer motivated to reach local customers can advertise and track results for less than what many people spend on their daily coffee fix. What can you achieve with these powerful tools at your fingertips?

Promotional Campaign Duration

The use of promotional campaigns is a proven method to capture data and generate interest in your products/services. Getting the timing of your promotional campaigns just right is a key to success. Here are a few general guidelines on how to set the timeframe for various promotional campaigns. Some marketers will want to avoid running campaigns too long, as the incentive to repeat visitors is reduced when they see the same promotion running all the time. If your goal is getting repeat traffic to your website, then keep it fresh!

Campaign Duration Guidelines

Types of Campaigns	Guidelines on Duration
Coupon	7-14 days
50% OFF	2-7 days
2-for-1 SPECIAL	2-7 days
$1000 Win Sweepstakes	30-60 days per campaign
Refer A Friend Incentive	Ongoing
Gift with Qualified Action	15-45 days
Self Liquidator	30-120 days
Instant Win Game	30-60 days
Scavenger Hunt	30-60 days

Creative Repetition and Brand Building

Before a consumer is likely to make a first-time purchase, a bond of trust must be established. This bond of trust is built through your efforts to solidify your Brand in the minds of the consumer.

As illustrated earlier, research shows that the average consumer needs to see a message seven times before they remember it. Once a Brand name, product or service name can be recalled, then typically a bond of trust is created, tearing down one of the largest obstacles for the Conversion Marketer.

To Achieve Brand awareness and recall, the best option is to create a campaign called "Creative Repetition." The Creative part is the message you choose to communicate, typically something simple and sometimes catchy in order to stick in the minds of consumers. The Repetition part is achieved by sending variations of your message several times over an appropriate period of time. The frequency of your email messages must be carefully timed to not burn-out your list, but not spaced out so long that your audience forgets the previous message.

Getting Results from a Data Capture Campaign

Now that you have potential customers opted-in to receive communications from you, what is the best path forward for driving conversion into revenue? In the next chapter, we explore psychological tools to help you achieve your conversion goals.

CLOSING THE SALE
HOW TO "ASK FOR THE
ORDER" ONLINE
Closing Defined

Anyone who has purchased a big-ticket item probably has a heightened appreciation for sales professionals, especially those with a finely tuned talent for the art of closing the deal. Such a professional is someone who highlights the features and benefits of a product. Then the skilled salesperson guides the customer to choose with their emotions, supporting the decision with facts. The result is a good purchase by a happy customer. This process seems almost effortless.

> *The skilled salesperson guides the customer to choose with their emotions, supporting the decision with facts.*

Unfortunately we all have been subjected to the negative side of sales as well. It comes in many forms. Picture a young couple on their honeymoon touring a posh resort. The timeshare industry is notorious for its hard-sell tactics. The couple may feel like they've been bound and gagged by the sales team, and they can't wait to leave the presentation. When was the last time your vacation was tainted by aggressive sales tactics from a timeshare operation?

Or remember the last time a telemarketer called you during dinner and you felt like they'd practically reached through the phone and taken hold of your ear (thank goodness for Caller ID). Think of a time you walked onto the lot of an auto dealership, all those shiny new models just begging for a test drive. But as soon as the salesman appeared over-eager, your defenses went up. "No thanks, just looking." Why do we do that? The reason is that people have a deep seated need not to be caught in the crosshairs as a sales target.

Sales and marketing professionals with relational skills are exceptionally talented at building trust and rapport with their customers. They have the ability to steer customers toward the best choice to fulfill their needs. Salespeople who cultivate the ability to ask for an order may dramatically accelerate their own career success and the success of a fast-growing company.

Excellent closing ratios create the revenue that is the lifeblood of all industry. Conversely, the toughest hurdle for a young salesperson to overcome is learning to ask for the order. They fear rejection or alienating the customer. This salesperson may not understand that a gentle nudge can save consumers from their own ambivalence. This can be a tough challenge for salespeople who have strong relational abilities.

These dynamics play into Conversion Marketing as well. As a Conversion Marketer, you'll want to guide your Interested Visitors toward the best choices. You'll want to enable a good purchase by a happy customer, with a process that seems almost effortless. In this chapter, you'll learn how to "ask for the order" in your online Conversion Marketing campaigns. It all begins with bridging the bond of trust.

Relationship Management

Let's take a look at one highly successful online Conversion Marketing campaign. This model illustrates how to ask for the order while simultaneously building a customer list and creating brand impressions. It also illustrates how a company with a large advertising budget can create an optimal Conversion Marketing campaign.

We'll start with the story of a salesman for an Internet advertising agency. We'll call him Sam. He was personally appealing; a young, tall Texan known for his fun-loving and engaging personality. Sam's clients loved being around him while on the job and after hours. He was quick to buy a drink, respectful to his clients, and he organized trips to special events. He'd take key decision makers to dinner or the golf course on a regular basis. Sam even provided clients with case studies to help build their personal career success.

In short, Sam was highly relational. He was exceptionally talented at building rapport and establishing relationships. Many of the key decision makers at prospect companies became his close personal friends. One such decision maker was an advertising buyer for Travelocity, the second largest online travel agency in the world. Yet in spite of Sam's great rapport with this key connection, he was afraid to ask for the sale. He didn't want to bruise the relationship he'd so carefully crafted with this key marketing executive. He didn't realize that he stood between his prospect and a fabulous marketing opportunity that the buyer really needed. By not asking for the sale, he was actually doing his client a disservice.

Ultimately, Travelocity did purchase a marketing campaign from the agency. Sam's boss had to fly in from another state to close the deal thereby impacting the agency's bottom line. And in a subtle way, it impacted Sam's own prestige with his client. Thanks to these early lessons in closing sales, Sam now enjoys a prestigious job with one of the top three online advertising companies in the world.

By asking for the order, everybody wins. Sam earns his commission. The agency wins a new client, and Travelocity enjoys the highest-performing marketing campaign in the history of the company. The same "win-win" principle applies to the art of asking for the order from your website. We will demonstrate how it works, but first let's take a look at the Travelocity success story in case you want to implement a similar strategy for your business.

Promotion

What Travelocity purchased from Sam is known as a Referral Marketing campaign, otherwise known as a Viral Marketing campaign defined earlier in the book. The idea is that the promotion spreads from person to person, like a virus. The only difference is that in online marketing terms, this person-to-person virus is a good thing.

Previously, we defined Promotion as an incentive campaign designed to stimulate or modify a consumer's short-term buying behavior. The reason that an online viral marketing or a referral marketing campaign works so well is that Word of Mouth advertising is the single-most effective form of advertising. With referral marketing, the recommendation to purchase a product comes from a trusted friend. The endorsement from a trusted friend helps bridge the bond of trust.

> *Word of Mouth advertising is the single-most effective form of advertising.*

The type of campaign Travelocity implemented was called a "Tell-A-Friend" campaign, with incentives given away as a reward for referring friends to register on the Travelocity website. The incentives had a high-appeal, yet because of Travelocity's size and positioning in the industry, it was not difficult for the company to produce these rewards. The prizes included one million frequent flyer miles to use for an exotic trip around the world, a BMW convertible, a golf vacation to the world-famous Pebble Beach golf resort in Northern California, plus coupons redeemed for discounted travel.

Here is how Travelocity's "Tell-A-Friend" campaign worked. Each consumer registering on the website earned one entry into a sweepstakes. After successfully registering, the consumer received an automatic auto-responder email, inviting them to tell their friends about the sweepstakes. The consumer was provided with a Referral Email to forward, telling their friends about the chance to win exotic prizes and earn valuable travel discounts. Each time a friend registered using the unique link embedded in the Referral Email, the referrer would earn additional entries into the sweepstakes plus earn increasingly valuable travel discount coupon codes – unique promotional codes that could be redeemed for travel discounts.

The travel coupons are an excellent example of how to ask for an order through a Conversion Marketing campaign. The more compelling the offer on the coupon, the more new Interested Visitors can be attracted. Here are some examples of coupon offers that historically generated the highest order rates:

- ✓ 2-for-1 offer: Get 2 products for the price of 1 (free companion airline ticket)

- ✓ 50% off special: always a strong performer

✓ Discount with Purchase: discount hotel coupons with the purchase of an airline ticket

So what are the techniques for asking for an order online? There are numerous methods, all of which depend on the profile of your company, your brand image, your products and pricing. For example, if you sell premium items such as Prada handbags, offering discount coupons would be inappropriate. The target audience for Prada will not necessarily respond to discount offers when shopping for the ultimate handbag, nor would couponing be consistent with the Prada brand image.

Image Matches Incentive

The first job is to evaluate the position of your brand image. The positioning of your brand image will determine in large part how you "ask for an order" online. High-end or luxury brands are best supported by imagery that supports the lifestyle to which you want your customers to aspire. Visit **www.Gucci.com** to see how they use imagery to support their brand position. Notice that the people who manage this brand will not ask for an order directly, however they will inspire you to DESIRE their brand using evocative imagery to stimulate your senses.

Buying Habits Match Frequency

Next, ask yourself how often your customers buy your products. If you sell frequently purchased products, such as items found in a typical drug store or grocery store, then sending periodic offers for your products is appropriate. If you sell an item like a Viking stove or a Sub-Zero refrigerator, that's a relatively expensive and infrequently purchased item, or a "considered purchase." In that case, providing great information such as product specifications, color choices, vivid imagery to create emotion and clever kitchen ideas will be a key ingredient to your success in driving conversions.

If you work in an industry offering frequent new products, then you'll want to create frequent communications to tell your audience about new products and discounts. An example of this is a company selling vacation packages like **www.ShermansTravel.com**, where there are hundreds of thousands of combinations of air/hotel/car-rental/cruise travel offers available each day.

Creating Urgency

Let's take a look at how a small company can successfully "ask for the order" online without spending tens of thousands of dollars on exotic vacations, cars, celebrity endorsement or complex marketing technology. One great method of asking for an order is offering price discounts. However instead of simply reducing your price, you want to create a sense of urgency to buy today. Creating urgency can be accomplished online using the techniques listed below:

8 Tools to Create Urgency

1. Free shipping with order (if you offer tangible products)

2. 2-for-1 offer

3. Percentage off with purchase (the amount of the discount will vary by your pricing strategy, but 50% off will generally generate the highest response rate).

4. Easy access to customer service through a toll-free phone number published prominently

5. An interactive chat session staffed by live operators

6. Offer a free download with purchase (such as an MP3 audio file, an eBook, research or video).

7. Scarcity – if you have limited inventory, show the customer how few of the items are available at any given moment.

8. Exitstitials – this is a term for a pop-up window that appears when a Visitor leaves your website or closes their browser with a "Last Chance to Buy" offer. It is a bit intrusive, but is also very effective.

A Case Study: Made For Success

Here is a method that is used to support the publishing business www.MadeForSuccess.com. This business sells audiobooks, books and ebooks from the top business minds in the world. Since less than one million people can recall the Made For Success brand, the company needs to build trust over time before asking for the order.

To accomplish this, Made For Success encourages visitors to register for a free weekly email newsletter with motivational and inspirational content targeted toward the desire to develop leadership skills. As an incentive to opt-in for the email newsletter, subscribers are given a free eBook or a 7-part ecourse.

Every two to three weeks, Made For Success promotes special offers on their product line. Here are blended examples from the Conversion Marketer's Toolbox and Conversion Tips to increase conversion:

- ✓ A risk-free, 30-day free trial offer (Unconditional Guarantee)

- ✓ Free eBooks from top authors (Gift with Purchase)

- ✓ Bonus motivational audio downloads (Buy 1, Get 1 Free)

- ✓ Bonus video content from world-class professional speakers such as Zig Ziglar, Jim Rohn and Bryan Tracy. This is an example of a Product Collections + The Draw of Authority

- ✓ Well written promotional copy with alluring imagery (Attractiveness Factor).

It is important to vary your special offers when asking for the sale, so as not to fatigue your audience with repetitiveness. At some stage, your audience will tune out recurring communications, so keep it FRESH!

EMAIL NEWSLETTERS
MONEY MAKING MAGIC

As this chapter is being written, it is a Friday. Today is the day I send my weekly email newsletter to thousands of subscribers. Why do I absolutely love this business? Today I am sitting in the sunshine on the shore of a mountain lake, which also has high-speed wireless Internet access. I am about to press the "Send" button on my weekly email newsletter to communicate with thousands of my customers, yet I am many miles from my "office."

A properly structured Internet business with automated Conversion Marketing campaigns set up enables anyone to work virtually anywhere . . . whether it is beside a beautiful mountain lake, on an exotic beach, aboard a cruise ship, in a bustling airport terminal or even from a quiet coffee shop.

Tomorrow morning I'll have a brand-new set of orders in my email Inbox, with the work to manage each incoming order 100% automated. Imagine for a moment what your lifestyle could be like if you could break free from the daily office routine to work when and where you choose. The possibilities are endless.

Let's explore the ins-and-outs of email marketing, where we'll talk about how to engage your Visitors' interests while simultaneously building the bond of trust. These are the fundamental mechanics of building a lasting relationship with your Visitors. It all starts with your email newsletter, or your ezine.

The beauty of mastering email marketing is that the average person can manage their list on their own. There's little need for specialized knowledge to put this information into practice. Once you are done reading this chapter, you will be equipped with the knowledge and resources to get started right away. With the tools available today, from spell checkers to self-editing email software, just about all you need to be successful at email marketing is a strong desire, quality content and consistency in communications.

The first step in the process is creating your email list. Two of the Promotional Tools covered earlier are perfect to use for building email lists: Games of Chance and Viral Marketing. A solid list is one of the greatest leverage points your e-business can have, second to traffic to your website. It is the foundation of your own success, and your email list is a valuable asset should you decide to sell your business. If you're going to sell goods or services, you'll need to have an email list to effectively sell.

Why build a list?

The first reason to build a solid mailing audience is Branding the company, products or services. Branding creates trust for consumers through repetition, as we've already covered. It's the same with ads on TV, radio or in print. Advertisers deliver the same message over and over. It takes multiple exposures to build recognition, then recognition turns to trust, then trust becomes desire, and desire becomes purchase.

Your ezine can generate three sources of revenue for your business:

1. Ecommerce – direct selling online

2. Subscription revenue

3. Advertising revenue from companies who advertise on your site

The saying goes, "The person with the biggest email list wins." It's a numbers game. You'll want to get as many website visitors as possible, convert them to email subscribers, then convert those subscribers into customers.

> "The person with the biggest email list wins."

Let's take a look at the components of a successful ezine. There are nine foundational elements to understand.

1. CONTENT:

The most tangible aspect of your newsletter is the content of your periodic communications. Your content strategy is what will keep people subscribed. By offering tips, suggestions and newsworthy items to your readers, they'll keep coming back to you. Creating content can be time-consuming, but content is the foundation of a good ezine.

Compelling content is the foremost reason why people visit a website and keep visiting in the future. As with any fast-moving business, there is more to learn than there are hours in the day. To help stay current, I retain an Internet Marketing specialist who advises me on ever-changing search-engine marketing strategies. He offered advice for an eCommerce company I operate, where we make regular blog posts and feature "How To" articles as a method of attracting first-time Visitors into our Conversions Loop.

Here are four content-oriented ideas to attract relevant traffic and build your email list:

1. Offer a free download incentive, such as MP3 audios or video when people opt-in to your email newsletter.

2. Create a research study to give away to each new opt-in.

3. Promote a discount off subsequent purchases (via a coupon) when you sign up for an email newsletter.

4. Provide access to a free library of content specific to your industry with each email opt-in.

2. THE HOOK

The less-tangle aspect of your ezine is called the "hook." Your hook is the reason someone chooses your ezine over any of the multitude of others they receive on a regular basis.

Consumers are inundated with email daily, so they are increasingly selective about what they take time to read. The hook must be relevant to your audience, and yet it must be different enough to attract and retain their attention. Take adequate time to create the perfect message around your hook. It is time well spent and will be leveraged many times over.

3. EMAIL BROADCAST TECHNOLOGY

You will want to engage a vendor for your email broadcast services. Find a good one who is reliable and has a reputation worthy of your business. There are numerous technology vendors catering to large corporations and small businesses alike. Different vendors cater to different-sized businesses. Perform a search on "email broadcast vendors," and you will discover plenty of options.

4. FREQUENCY OF COMMUNICATION

The frequency of your email communications must be regular and predictable in the eyes of your consumer. The graphics you use in your email, if any, must be consistent with the graphics on your website. How often you publish your newsletters must also be regular/uniform. Choose a specific day of the week to send out your communiqué, and stick to that schedule. This is key to establishing trust and credibility in the eyes of your audience.

Here are a few guidelines in establishing your schedule. A decent starting point is a weekly frequency, but there are tradeoffs given the time it takes to send a weekly email broadcast. Receiving email once per month is long time, from a consumer viewpoint; your competition will likely contact potential customers several times a month to achieve top-of-mind awareness.

Scheduling daily email broadcasts to your opt-in lists is perfect for some companies, but can be overkill if your information is not highly valuable to the consumer. With email volumes rising dramatically each year, email communications can become diluted, while what we call "list fatigue" sets in due to over communication. Unless your messaging is directly relevant to accomplishing the needs of your target audiences, then a daily email frequency may get read once then automatically deleted or ignored upon subsequent messages.

Your messaging needs to be highly relevant and pertinent to the needs of your audience. As you understand the costs of acquiring each new opt-in to the Conversions Loop, the last thing you can afford is to have your branding messages get ignored because they are deemed irrelevant.

The types of messages that can be relevant for daily communication are those messages that are critical for daily operations, needed industry news, financial information or other rapidly changing information. Examples of daily email messaging that works include financial information, breaking news, daily motivation or inspiration from trusted sources, rapidly changing price data, or other timely information used to make key decisions.

Email frequency planning also depends on your access to content. If you're writing the content, plan to budget a specific amount of time for this activity. You can write the content yourself if your subscribers are attracted to your unique point of view or force of personality. As an alternative, you may want to receive editorial contributions from other writers in your industry.

There are many authors and content providers who agree to provide content for free or sometimes for a small fee. To negotiate free content, offer credit for the writer's contribution in the ezine by publishing their bio and adding a link to their website. This has proven to be a powerful manner in which content providers drive traffic to their websites.

Email can be one of the most effective Conversion tools at your disposal. Here are some principles of Email Marketing frequency to achieve long-term success in communicating the value of your products/services.

Email Frequency Guidelines

TYPES OF PRODUCTS / SERVICES	EMAIL FREQUENCY Suggestions	DURATION
Transactional products	Weekly	Ongoing
"Considered" purchases	Weekly	Limited, based on the typical buying cycle for your product/service
Luxury/Premium products	Monthly or Event driven	Ongoing
Wholesale/Commercial	Depends on the frequency of Purchase Orders	Ongoing
Promotional Campaign	Semi-weekly or Weekly	30-day duration

5. EMAIL FORMATTING

Your software should allow you to create and distribute your ezine as elegantly as possible. Ezines can be formatted in either of two ways, HTML (a form of program code called Hyper-Text Mark-up Language) or plain text.

There is ongoing debate about which form is the most effective in generating eCommerce. Plain text, because it appeals to the lowest common denominator in terms of technology, undoubtedly reaches the most consumers. Everyone can access plain text, so your carefully crafted words are read by more people. But that doesn't necessarily translate to higher conversion rates. People are visually oriented, and buying habits are directly attributable to the Attraction Factor. If you have a premium Brand or product, consider using rich imagery in your email communications to better relay an emotion associated with your Brand.

With HTML, the look is more deluxe. Results appear more like a web page, and can include graphics, photos, audio and even video.

There is a third choice, and that is a technology called a "web sniffer." Many software vendors have technology that automatically distributes your ezine for you and literally decides on the fly whether a subscriber's email account can handle HTML or if their email account requires plain text.

Ultimately the format you choose depends on three factors.

1. Your audience – to whom are you communicating?

2. Your message – what kind of content are you sending?

3. Your bottom line – what kind of results are you seeking?

Track these factors to decide what yields the best results for you. Knowledge is power. For my purposes, I elected to format newsletters graphically in the HTML format. The software used to support my business helps with the formatting through easy-to-use templates. My ultimate goals are branding and eCommerce conversions, and the use of images has been effective in achieving these goals.

6. TRACKING & REPORTING

Most software vendors have robust email-tracking tools at their fingertips to track all data associated with distribution. Every eCommerce enterprise will want to understand these basic tracking numbers to evaluate how its communications are performing. The numbers tell a story and create a gauge of the effort going into email marketing.

   a)   Number of active subscribers
The first thing you want to know is how many people you're reaching. If your sales are not meeting your goals, this is a great place to start making enhancements.

b) Open Rates
Open Rates refer to the number of people who open your ezine and take a look at the content.

Let's take a look at some of the influences on why a customer chooses whether to ready what you send. The Subject Line of your email establishes your ezine's relevance to what your subscriber is seeking. Keep it catchy, but appropriate to your content.

Open Rates are also influenced by how busy the subscriber is that day. The Open Rates will vary depending on such factors as the day of the week sent, the time of the day sent, even whether your message was sent during a holiday week.

As a general rule, the best days to send an ezine are Monday through Thursday. On Saturday and Sunday, there is a drop-off rate for Internet usage because most people are not at work – where they most commonly check their email. Monday is a less-favorable day for sending ezines because subscribers are inundated by emails sent over the weekend.

Content relevancy will determine whether your email gets opened. If you provide content that they need first thing Monday morning, it will vault your readership over the competition. Fridays traditionally have lower open rates for many businesses as people work from home, take three-day weekends, or work four, ten-hour days during the week with Fridays off. However, it can be wise to broadcast on days which are the least competitive in terms of email mindshare.

c) Click-through Rates
This is the number of subscribers who not only open your ezine, but also click on one or more links embedded in your content. Based on research data from 65,000 small businesses, the average click-through rate is 8.9%. The best items to feature to ensure click-throughs are coupons, incentives and weblinks to your own website to promote direct sales.

d) Undeliverable and Bounce Rates
Causes for undeliverable email include full mailboxes or outdated email addresses. People go through about two or three email addresses per year. They receive so much unsolicited advertising, or SPAM, many

choose to abandon an email address rather than comb through the messages.

e)   Unsubscribes

This is the number-per-reporting period of people requesting to be removed from your distribution list. This typically is managed automatically by an Email Software Vendor. If your Unsubscribe rates increase, you may examine your Content strategy or your Frequency strategy (over communication to your list is a big reason for Unsubscribes).

f)   Referrals

This is also called Tell a Friend. An average of 3.3% of subscribers will take advantage of referral offers (without incentives). This rate may sound a little low to you. Even so, word-of-mouth is the most powerful form of advertising.

7.   COMPLIANCE WITH THE CAN-SPAM ACT

The CAN-SPAM Act passed by the U.S. Government in 2001 creates requirements that all legitimate email distributors must comply. If a company or individual is not complying with the published guidelines, they could face financial penalties in a court of law.

The purpose of the Act is to reduce SPAM or unsolicited email in circulation. Any email sent must follow accepted permission-based email guidelines. Prohibited are the uses of web crawlers, spiders or robots. These are software programs that comb websites for email addresses then add them to a bulk mailing list. Typical offerings from vendors who use web crawlers include mortgages, online gambling, software discounts and pharmaceutical offers.

In order to comply with the CAN-SPAM Act, you need to have an automated method to unsubscribe from your distribution list. Also having a subscription log with dates and IP (Internet Protocol is the number assigned to a computer) addresses will help protect you in case someone forgets they subscribed to your ezine. Having a history will resolve any question if the issue of SPAM arises.

Another issue you'll need to comply with is a method of contact. Make sure your emails provide a way to reach you, including an email address, a phone number, or a post office box. Spammers often conceal their identities, making it tough to get off their lists.

You will also want to be sure to have a privacy policy. The Direct Marketing Association offers an online wizard on their website to help draft your own privacy policy. For more information, go to **www.theDMA.org**. The wizard allows you to select options about your business activities and translate that into a written privacy policy.

Once you draft your privacy policy, you need to make sure your data practices are in compliance with your policy. Fundamental to this policy is how you choose to use the data you collect from website Visitors.

For added security, you will want to run your completed ezine through a SPAM filter, such as Spam Assassin. The software will check your content to ensure that you are compliant with the CAN-SPAM Act.

In spite of regulations, some companies continue to use SPAM in their marketing practices. Internet Service Providers (ISPs), facing a huge volume of complaints, now use SPAM filters to block unwanted emails for their subscribers. You want to make sure that, as a legitimate emailer, you are able to get through the SPAM filters.

There are many triggers for SPAM filters, and unfortunately the one that tops the list is also the most powerful word in marketing: free. This will trip a SPAM filter almost every time, so be careful. You may want to use a synonym or alternative formatting, such as F.R.E.E. Other keywords to caution against include sweepstakes, pharmaceutical, Viagra, mortgage, investment and special offer (especially when used in the Subject Line of email broadcasts).

Finally, to comply with the CAN-SPAM Act, you'll want to consider taking advantage of offering Double Opt-in to new subscribers. This is an expressed request by a consumer to subscribe to your email list. Have consumers go to your website and complete a brief form in order to subscribe, or Opt-In.

Using Double Opt-in typically includes an auto-responder to immediately send an email with an embedded link back to your website. Their subscription is only active once they have confirmed their interest by clicking on this link. This Double Opt-In technique prevents mistakes or malicious pranks by third parties, and it saves everyone a bit of hassle.

Be aware that using the Double Opt-In reduces subscription rates by as much as 25% (effectively increasing your cost per subscriber by 25%), yet it also creates a more solid and reliable email list. You can also use website redundancy or an email reply instead of the email click-through process just described.

8. LIST BUILDING

List building activities are an important aspect of your Conversion Marketing planning, warranting your time and focus. Here are 7 essential tips to get the process started as you develop strategies to grow your lists:

    a)   Website sign-up form

This form is a fill-in the blanks questionnaire on a website which invites Visitors to engage with your company. A sign-up form is frequently found on a Home Page and many other pages on a website. Consider using incentives to entice Visitors to sign up when they visit your website for the first time.

    b)   Offline

Sign-up sheets: If you speak at conferences, have attendees sign up at the back of the room or pass around an email sign-up sheet. The same strategy applies to retailers, event photographers, hotels and just about any other business with an offline presence.

c) Purchase advertising

Buying ad banners on other websites to drive email newsletter sign-ups is a common practice. Closely monitor your cost per acquisition when buying online advertising.

d) Pay-per-click (PPC)

PPC inventory is a popular form of advertising you can purchase by identifying keywords used on major search engines, portals or ad networks. You only pay when a Visitor comes to your website, so make sure that the message in your advertising is very specific to what you want Visitors to do when they visit your website.

e) Email List Rental

Renting an email list from another company is one of the quickest methods to build your email list. With this option, you transmit your prepared promotional message to a company who has agreed to distribute it for you one time for a fee, typically negotiated through a List Broker.

A typical rate for such a service would be $100 per 1,000 names, or $100 CPM (cost per thousand). The company you rent the names from does not actually provide you with names; they only send the email for you. It's the consumer's responsibility to visit your site and Opt-In if they would like to be a subscriber.

f) Co-registration

Co-Registration, or Co-Reg as the industry insiders call it, is where one website may offer other businesses the opportunity to share information every time someone signs up on the site. The cost for the buyer who uses co-registration may be a cost effective $.10-$.50 cents per name in your database, depending on the relevance of the email address to your target audience.

g) List Swap

Creating list-swap partnerships are one of my personal favorite methods to grow email lists. If you have a large email list, you can use this as leverage to trade lists with companies with equally large lists. This brings us back to the concept, "The one with the biggest email list wins!"

9. How to make money with your Email List

If you're going to invest time and money building your email list, many people want to clearly know how they can use that list to generate revenue. Here is a summary of four commonsense methods to maximize your investment in email:

a) Branding – using your ezine to establish your brand in the mind of your consumer is paramount to build trust, which we established is key to the Conversion Marketing cycle. Ultimately, your email list will be the conduit to generating revenues via product and service sales.

b) Affiliate Marketing – promoting Affiliate offers to your ezine subscribers is a proven method to generate passive income from your ezine. Affiliates will pay a commission percentage from purchases on their websites when your subscribers buy from Affiliates. Conversions are tracked using Affiliate Management software used by your Affiliate partners.

c) Advertising –companies with larger lists will run ads in their ezine in exchange for advertising revenue. The pricing you charge can be based on a Cost per Thousand basis (CPM) or Pay-per-Click (PPC), and varies depending on the industry. To generate meaningful sales revenues, email list owners may hire a dedicated sales force, work with a list brokers or simply sell their inventory online. Some email publishers populate their ezines with ads provided by advertising networks (like Google AdWords), which pay the publisher each time someone clicks on an ad published on their website.

d) Email List Rental – Renting your list to third parties who send a dedicated message to your subscribers is a method used by large list owners. Many consumers elect to receive information about related new products and services.

You may be wondering how many names you should target to have in your list. What's a good number to strive for? The answer is that it depends on a lot of factors, and the possibilities are almost endless. A business-to-business company may be thrilled to have 250 names on their list. A smaller consumer-oriented company may thrive on a solid, well-groomed list of 10,000 names. A national brand would likely be unimpressed with such a number and will need hundreds of thousands, or millions of names, before they would consider their list a success.

One key ingredient in determining the size of your list is the amount of money budgeted on advertising. You'll want to take a look at your cost per acquisition and see if you're getting your money's worth for your list-building activities.

Another factor you might examine is how many names you're gathering at special events. How many speaking engagements do you do in a year? How many trade shows do you attend? These are arenas on which to focus in order to strongly promote, and effectively enhance your subscriber base.

The bottom line is that whether you're involved in eCommerce or a brick-and-mortar business, a strong online newsletter creates buzz and generates cashflow.

CONCLUDING REMARKS

Hear that little hum? That's the sound of the wheels of commerce growing by leaps and bounds each year. Are you getting your fair share of the hundreds of billions spent each year on eCommerce?

Implementing these best promotional marketing practices in your eCommerce endeavors will yield rich dividends in your business. Keep this book near your desk as a handy reference tool for years to come. For more resources, visit **www.ConversionMarketingBook.com** for fresh ideas, printable resources from this book and inspiration for your marketing campaigns.

Put these Conversion Marketing principles into action and put a fully automated, silent sales-professional to work for your business.

Good selling!

Bryan Heathman has built email databases with millions of subscribers and has consulted with clients, and their agencies, including NISSAN Motors, Proctor & Gamble, Travelocity, TV Guide and numerous New York Times best-selling authors.

Bryan is a featured speaker at associations such as the National Speakers Association (NSA), Photographic Marketing Association (PMA), American Marketing Association (AMA), National Speakers Association (NSA) and Direct Marketing Association (DMA).

Mr. Heathman holds a BS Degree in Economics and has worked for Fortune 100 companies including Microsoft, Xerox and Eastman Kodak Company. He lives in Seattle and can be found on the tennis court or playing jazz in his spare time.

To contact Mr. Heathman for speaking engagements, corporate consulting or questions about your online promotional strategy, visit **www.BryanHeathman.com** for information or call his office at 425-526-6480.

AUDIO *Ink*
PUBLISHING

AudioInk Publishing was founded on the principle that "everyone has a story to tell".

"You tell the story, we tell the world"

AudioInk Publishing, a division of Made For Success, Inc., is dedicated to providing authors and speakers the opportunity to "Tell their story" through the ever expanding methods of publishing, from physical books to mobile apps. We provide generous royalties for self-published authors and speakers in an effort to extend the greatest opportunity to all we have the honor of serving.

There are many ways we can assist you with your book project:

1. From getting your manuscript started to manuscript editing, we can help you get your manuscript to print.

2. If you are in the process of writing a book, ask about the **Writers Academy** training course for new authors. You'll learn amazing and time-saving secrets to getting your book written and published.

3. The "Publisher of the Future" is part Ad Agency and part Publisher. From Book Trailer videos to book websites, we have the marketing solution for every budget. Contact us to plan a Best Seller marketing campaign for your book.

4. Book Derivatives: We're experts at many types of unique and new book publishing options. We specialize in the basics of a print book, an eBook or an audiobook, to the "book of the future" delivered as a mobile app.

Visit www.AudioInk.com to read testimonials and see sample book marketing campaigns. Give us a call at 1-888-884-8365 x5 or send us a note at **sales@AudioInk.com**

Get Quantity Discounts

AudioInk Published Print books are available at quantity discounts for orders of 10 copies or more. Please call us toll free at (888)-884-8365 or email us at support@AudioInk.com

Lightning Source UK Ltd.
Milton Keynes UK
UKOW05f1150241016

286000UK00001B/258/P